NIGERIA, UNITED KINGDOM AND REPUBLIC OF IRELAND:
a Book of Profiles

Publisher's note
Every possible effort has been made to ensure that the information contained in this book is accurate at the time of going to press, and the publishers and author cannot accept responsibility for any errors or omissions, however caused. No responsibility for loss or damage occasioned to any person acting, or refraining from action, as a result of the material in this publication can be accepted by the editor, the publisher or the author/compiler.

First published in Great Britain in 2018 under the title: *Nigerian-British Politicians in the United Kingdom and Republic of Ireland: A book of profiles*

Due acknowledgement is made with thanks, for materials (texts and images) used from the personal, political party and borough council websites in relation to the profiled.

Enquiries relating to sales, marketing and distribution should be sent to the publishers:
Leading Management Publishing
74 Church Road
London
SE19 2EZ
+44 (0) 7972 22 80 90
ade.aminu@yahoo.co.uk
www.diasporanpolitics.com

© **Adedamola Aminu, 2018**

The right of Adedamola Aminu to be identified as the Author/Compiler of this work has been asserted in accordance with the Copyright, Designs and Patents Act 1988

British Library Cataloguing in Publication Data
A CIP record for this book is available from the British Library
ISBN **978-1-9999650-0-6**

Typeset/Design/Editorial/Publishing Consultants
Infomediaworks Ltd
+44 (0) 7474 163 745
admin@infomediaworks.co.uk
www.infomediaworks.co.uk

Printed and bound by CPI Group (UK) Ltd, Croydon CR0 4YY

Dedication

This book is dedicated to my children: **Olanrewaju, Omotayo, Boluwatife, Oyindamola** and **Adeolu**. You are trusted and worthy companions, co-travellers in life's epic journey. I will always cherish you. Much love!

Also for my mother, **Mrs Wulemotu Abegbe Aminu**:
Mama, thank you for life's lessons. You provided a solid foundation for me and taught me to love humanity. Your kindness and fair disposition lighted my path.

…my sister, **Mrs Oladunni Oderinde**, who has been a significant part of my life and personal development….

…and to **Adedolapo Aminu**
You are a shining beacon of hope, a solid pillar of support and without an iota of doubt, my most trusted confidant.

Acknowledgements

I would like to express my gratitude to the numerous people whose individual and collective efforts enabled the successful completion of this book. My thanks go to the different strands of professionals who provided the necessary support by reading the manuscripts, offering ideas and useful comments to improve both the content and the context of the publication. I acknowledge the sound professional input that has gone into the editing, proofreading and the design of the book.

The support from my colleague councillors and our honourable MPs who promptly responded to my request to have their profiles published is hugely appreciated. Others who were hard pressed for time have kindly allowed materials to be used from their websites. To all of these patriots, I say a big thank you.

I would also like to thank my friend and publishing consultant, Segun Martins Fajemisin, for his support and encouragement in urging me to publish this book of profiles.

My sincere appreciation goes to my constituents for entrusting me with a mandate to serve them. Without you, even this project would not have materialised. Your kindness and support made this a possibility.

Above all, I want to thank my wife, Dolapo, and the rest of my family, who supported and encouraged me despite the fact that the project took a lot of my time, most of which I would have loved to spend in their company. To have their support in the course of the journey was invaluable.

And to those friends and associates whose names I have not been able to list due to the constraints of time and space, thank you so much for all your contributions and continued support. God bless you.

Cllr. Adedamola Aminu *B.A. (Hons), Dip.M, M.A, PGCE (Cant)*
Councillor, Tulse Hill Ward, Brixton, Borough of Lambeth
Chairman Association of British-Nigerian Councillors
President, Association of Nigerian Academics UK

CONTENTS

DEDICATION 3
ACKNOWLEDGEMENTS 5
PREFACE 13
INTRODUCTION 17

ROLE OF MEMBER OF PARLIAMENT (MP) 21
MS CHI ONWURAH MP 24
MRS HELEN GRANT MP 25
KATE OSAMOR MP 27
CHUKA UMUNNA MP 28
FIONA ONASANYA MP 29
BIM AFOLAMI MP 30
KEMI BADENOCH MP 31

ROLE OF THE MAYORS/SPEAKERS 33

PAST AND CURRENT MAYORS/ 37
SPEAKERS OF NIGERIAN HERITAGE
CLLR JANET ADEGOKE 38
CLLR ERELU LOLA AYONRINDE 38
CLLR AFOLASADE BRIGHT 38
CLLR ROTIMI ADEBARI 38
CLLR EMMANUEL OBASOHAN 39
CLLR ANNA MBACHU 39
CLLR TAYO SITU 39
CLLR SUSAN FAJANA-THOMAS 39
CLLR KATE ANOLUE 40
CLLR MICHAEL ADEYEYE 40
CLLR IRENE FASEYI 40
CLLR ADEDAMOLA AMINU 40
CLLR MERCY UMEH 41
CLLR OBAJIMI ADEFIRANYE 41
CLLR DONATUS ANYAWU 41
CLLR SADE ETTI 41

CLLR PAT EKECHI 42
CLLR OLUGBENGA BABATOLA 42
CLLR TUNDE OJETOLA 42
CLLR YEMI OSHO 42
CLLR SORAYA ADEJARE 43

ROLE OF COUNCILLORS 45

BARKING & DAGENHAM BOROUGH 47
CLLR EMMANUEL OBASOHAN 48
CLLR JAMES OGUNGBOSE 48
COUNCILLOR AFOLASADE BRIGHT 48
CLLR ADEGBOYEGA OLUWOLE 51
CLLR SANCHIA ALASIA 51

BEXLEY BOROUGH 54
CLLR ENDY EZENWATA 55
CLLR MABEL OGUNDAYO 56

BRENT BOROUGH 57
CLLR MICHAEL ADEYEYE 58
CLLR TAYO OLADAPO 59
CLLR ERNEST NNAAMA EZEAJUGHI 59
CLLR AISHA ENIOLA 60
CLLR BENJAMIN OLUKAYODE OGUNRO 61

ENFIELD BOROUGH 62
CLLR KATE NDIDI ANOLUE 63
CLLR. (MS) NNEKA KEAZOR.. 66
CLLR OZZIE UZOANYA 68
CHIEF COUNCILLOR PATRICIA CHINYERE NMAKU EKECHI (NEE ANAH).. 68

GREENWICH BOROUGH 71
CLLR OLUGBENGA BABATOLA....................................... 72
CLLR TONIA ASHIKODI (MS) 73

CONTENTS

HACKNEY BOROUGH 75
CLLR SUSAN FAJANA-THOMAS 76
CLLR MICHAEL JONES 77
CLLR SADE ETTI 79
CLLR SORAYA ADEJARE 81
CLLR KAM ADAMS 82

HAMMERSMITH & FULHAM BOROUGH 83
CLLR MERCY UMEH 84
CLLR MRS. JANET ADEGOKE 84

HARINGEY BOROUGH 86
CLLR CHARLES ADJE 87
CLLR JOSEPH EJIOFOR 88
CLLR MARTHA OSAMOR 89

HARROW BOROUGH 91
CLLR CHIKA AMADI 92

HAVERING BOROUGH 94
CLLR WILLIAM ODULATE 95

LAMBETH BOROUGH 96
CLLR ADEDAMOLA AMINU 97
CLLR DONATUS ANYANWU 99
CLLR FLORENCE ESHALOMI 100
CLLR LINDA BELLOS 101
CLLR AMANDA INYANG 103
CLLR ÀBÁYÒMÍ BURAIMOH-IGBO 103

LEWISHAM BOROUGH 104
CLLR CRADA ONUEGBU 105
CLLR OBAJIMI ADEFIRANYE 105
CLLR RACHEL ONIKOSI 106
CLLR OLUROTIMI OGUNBADEWA 106
CLLR SAMUEL OWOLABI-OLUYOLE 107

Nigerian-British Politicians in United Kingdom
and Republic of Ireland: a book of Profiles

CLLR ANNE AFFIKU.. 107
CLLR JOSEPH FOLORUNSO 108
CLLR OLUFUNKE ABIDOYE 108
TAYO OKE 108

MERTON BOROUGH..**109**
CLLR GREGORY PATRICK UDEH 110
CLLR FIDELIS GADZAMA 110

MILTON KEYNES BOROUGH 111
CLLR TUBO URANTA... 111

NEWHAM BOROUGH.. 112
CLLR JOY LAGUDA MBE 113
CLLR CHARITY FIBERESIMA 113
CLLR SEYI AKINWOWO... 114
CLLR SIMEON ADEWOLE ADEMOLAKE 115

SOUTHWARK BOROUGH 118
CLLR TAYO SITU... 119
CLLR MICHAEL SITU 120
CLLR THE RIGHT REVEREND EMMANUEL OYEWOLE 120
CLLR MICHAEL BUKOLA 122
CLLR SUNNY LAMBE... 123
CLLR JOHNSON SITU 125
CLLR JAMES OKOSUN 126
CLLR ADEDOKUN LASAKI 126
CLLR OLAJUMOKE RISIKAT OYEWUNMI 127
CLLR JELIL LADIPO 127
ABDUR-RAHMAN O. OLAYIWOLA 127

WALTHAM FOREST BOROUGH 128
CLLR ANNA MBACHU.. 129
ELIZABETH ATINUKE ADEBUTU 130
CLLR WHITNEY IHENACHOR 132
CLLR YEMI OSHO 132
CLLR BABTUNDE DAVIES-ADEBUTU 135

CONTENTS

WANDSWORTH BOROUGH 137
HON. ALDERMAN ERELU LOLA AYONRINDE 138

WESTMINSTER BOROUGH 139
CLLR DAVID OBAZE 140

DISTRICT COUNCILS 141

BRACKNELL FOREST BOROUGH COUNCIL 142
CLLR MICHAEL ADENIYI GBADEBO 143

CHESHIRE EAST COUNCIL 145
CLLR IRENE FASEYI 145

HERTSMERE BOROUGH COUNCIL 146
CLLR VICTOR O ENI 146

LEWES DISTRICT COUNCIL 147
CLLR SAM ADENIJI 147

MANCHESTER CITY COUNCIL 148
COUNCILLOR TUTU EKO (PRINCE) 148

MEDWAY COUNCIL 150
COUNCILLOR GLORIA OPARA 150
CLLR HABEEB ADEYEMI HAROLD OGUNFEMI 151

NOTTINGHAM CITY COUNCIL 153
CLLR LESLIE AYOOLA 153
CLLR PATIENCE ULOMA IFEDIORA 154

OXFORD CITY COUNCIL 156
CLLR BEN LLOYD-SHOGBESAN 157

SEVENOAKS DISTRICT COUNCIL 158
CLLR ANGELA GEORGE 158
CLLR ELIZABETH KOMOLAFE 159

THURROCK COUNCIL 160
CLLR TUNDE OJETOLA 161
CLLR BUKKY OKUNADE 162

WATFORD BOROUGH COUNCIL 164
CLLR FAVOUR EWUDO 164

WOLVERTON AND GREENLEYS TOWN COUNCIL 165
CLLR ADEBAYO MURISIKU FASINRO 165
CLLR MUNIR BAKARE 166

WYCOMBE DISTRICT COUNCIL 168
CLLR SHADE ADOH 169

THE REPUBLIC OF IRELAND 171
ROTIMI ADEBARI 171

CONCLUSION 175

Preface

> "*If you don't blow your own horn,
> someone else will use it as a spittoon.*"
> - **Kenneth H. Blanchard,**
> *American author and management expert*

We now live in a world which is increasingly tethered on competition, and with too many influences battling for the observer's attention. Choices have to be made, and lessons learnt in as little time as possible and within a plethora of choices. So, it pays to blow your horn or highlight your positive sides.

Modesty nonetheless remains a virtue, but who can fault sensible efforts geared toward the highlight and celebration of laudable achievements? It is expedient on our part to leave a positive notion for posterity and for the coming generations to aspire to and transcend.

In the views of Blanchard, those who refuse to do this risk confining laudable achievements to the pits of obliviousness. A '*spittoon*' is a receptacle for spit, usually in a public place.

With this at the fore, the idea of publishing a profile of Nigerian-British community politicians becomes highly desirable. This book of profile documents both serving and former Members of Parliament (MPs), Mayors and Councillors. At the risk of tautology, I dare say that Nigeria is a land blessed with abundant human and material resources. And this is a fact. It is the reason that her people will strive and eventually achieve excellence, even when confronted with starkness and a daunting propensity to fail. It also explains why dignity, enterprise and resourcefulness have distinguished us among peoples of other descents.

It is with such illustriousness and pride that some people have not only seen the need for participation in shaping policies that affect our community, but such efforts have also been geared towards empowering the community and offering them a voice in the political arena.

There are over fifty councillors of Nigerian descent currently sitting in the various councils in the United Kingdom. These range from Lambeth to Enfield and as far as Thurrock and Cambridge.

Also, it is on record that there have been twenty-one elected councillors to serve as Mayors in different boroughs. Also, worthy of mention is the fact that whenever they have been elected Mayor, Nigerian-Britons' are always the first of such BME appointments to have thus taken place.

Posterity will justify the positioning of this publication, more especially at a time when the need has arisen for a new generation of politicians and administrators to mount the saddle both at home and abroad.

It is therefore with great delight and enthusiasm that I commend this book of profiles to you. While blowing one's horn may not have adequately captured the essence of the project, I take delight in the fact that a book has been published that is not only a pioneering effort but that which may serve as a pivot for future referential endeavours.

Nigeria continues to project greatness at all fronts, and well-meaning citizens wherever they are, continue to aspire to lofty placement for themselves and their offspring. Leaving a laudable trail that is worthy of emulation is great. But greater still would be the commitment that will emanate if a new generation of community advocates would have been inspired by the modest achievements of the forerunners such as this book has outlined.

Segun Martins Fajemisin
Publishing / Media / Consulting

Introduction

The UK democracy offers a dynamic socio-political system highly esteemed around the world. Much revered for its multiculturalism and diversity, it has built into the structure a veritable and all-embracing party-political system favourably disposed to the growth of politicians at all tiers of government, including the local government.

Nigerian-British councillors, MPs and GLA members elected to serve on the Council, Parliament and Greater London Assembly level have thus grown in number over the years with added roles and responsibilities accorded them in representative governance. In a move to support on-going efforts to celebrate those hard-working councillors, MPs and GLA representatives who are contributing in the realm of nation-building, this publication has taken aim at profiling Nigerian-British politicians across all the registered parties in the United Kingdom.

A concise but insightful description of individuals who have so distinguished themselves by working hard to integrate into the body politic of the United Kingdom governance system and structure, the book will also highlight the different project areas with which the individual politician is engaged.

The purpose of this book is to document the involvement in, and modest contributions of Nigerians to the British political system.

The book will look at when a Nigerian was first elected in a representative capacity and the subsequent elections of Nigerians to political offices by outlining Councillors, Mayors, Member of Parliament and Assembly members.

The benchmark for being listed is when councillors were first elected, and not how many times they have sought to be elected and failed. The pioneering efforts of these office holders deserve documentation for posterity. We have the landmark achievement of the first woman Nigerian-British council leader, Linda Bellos, who was elected on the Labour Party platform in Lambeth London Borough Council in 1986. She served in this position till 1988.

What of the first male Nigerian-British Council leader Charles Adje, elected in Haringey in 2004. He served in this position till 2006.

Nigerian-Britons' integration and participation in UK politics could be traced to the first such elected councillor in 1978. As listed in the London Borough Council Elections 4 May 1978 returns, Mr William A. Odulate was elected under the Conservative Party platform for the Chase Cross (Romford) district of the London Borough of Havering.

The first Nigerian-Briton to be elected Mayor was Mrs Janet O. Adegoke (Labour) elected 10th May 1986 for Starch Green (Hammersmith) in the London Borough of Hammersmith and Fulham.

These forerunners have, in their modest ways, paved the way for the next and current generations of politicians in their respective boroughs. This book of profiles stands, therefore, to fill in the role of a reference book for the general public, and for both the current and future generations of Nigerian-Britons aspiring to serve their community.

The challenges with which this project was beset are varied and multi-dimensional. Firstly, data relating to the ethnic minorities were never mined or analysed by country of origin – every black person in the UK political realm is classified as African-Caribbean! Thus, to arrive at any collation, a form of benchmark had to be set, especially where pertinent data on personal details are as sparse as the subjects.

To start with, in identifying Nigerians who have thus been elected into service, a viable means of identification is the name. Once identified by name, the researcher then goes to dig deep into the related historical details of, say, the councillor. Despite the inherent limitation of missing out on councillors of Nigerian descent whose nomenclature may not have given away their land of birth, it is hoped that this pioneering effort will be able to build on a modest success and include emerging information as updates in future editions. This is a must if the publication must fulfil its referential purpose as well as staying true to being a veritable documentation of historical facts. And this is a task the publishers are prepared to take heads on.

It is hoped that this publication will lend itself to projecting the image of the Nigerian community as well as documenting the modest, yet laudable achievements of the individual MPs, GLA and Councillors for posterity. It will also aim to present to the world another positive side of our dynamic community.

Further to the above point, it is expected that the magnitude and dimension of the publication will equally serve as a source of inspiration to others who may aspire to serve in this capacity in the future.

Cllr. Adedamola Aminu

ROLE OF MEMBER OF PARLIAMENT (MP)

The UK is divided into 650 areas called constituencies. During an election, everyone eligible to cast a vote in a constituency selects one candidate to be their MP. The candidate who gets the most votes becomes the MP for that area until the next election.

General elections
At a general election, all constituencies become vacant and a Member of Parliament is elected for each from a list of candidates standing for election. General elections happen every five years. If an MP dies or retires, a bye-election is held in that constituency to find new MP for that area.

Political parties
The UK Parliament has MPs from areas across England, Scotland, Wales and Northern Ireland. In addition, there is a Parliament in Scotland, a National Assembly in Wales and a National Assembly in Northern Ireland.

Separate elections are held for these devolved political bodies which have been granted powers on a regional level that the UK

Parliament was formerly responsible for. Candidates who win seats in these elections do not become MPs in the UK Parliament. Most MPs are members of one of the five main political parties in the UK - *Labour, Conservative, Liberal Democrat, Green* and *UKIP*. In Wales, Scotland and Northern Ireland they also have other parties such as *Scottish National Party, Plaid Cymru, DUP, Sinn Fein* and *Ulster Unionist Party*. Other MPs represent smaller parties or are independent of a political party.

To become an MP representing a main political party, a candidate must be authorised to do so by the party's nominating officer. They must then win the most votes in the constituency to be a candidate.

The general public in the UK who is 18 or above elects Members of Parliament (MPs) to represent their interests and concerns in the House of Commons every five years.

MPs consider and can propose new laws as well as raising issues that matter to you in the House. This includes asking government ministers questions about current issues including those which affect local constituents.

MPs divide their time between working in Parliament and working in their constituency that elected them and working for their political party.

Some MPs from the governing party (or parties) may become government ministers with specific responsibilities in certain areas, such as Education, Business, Health, Transport, Defence, Housing etc. MPs also work in their constituency in addition to their role in Government or Parliament, they will still continue to hold regular surgeries to help their constituents.

Working in Parliament
When Parliament is sitting, MPs generally spend their time working in the House of Commons. This includes raising issues affecting their constituents, attending debates and voting on new laws. This can either be by asking a question of a government minister on your behalf or supporting and highlighting particular campaigns which local people feel strongly about.

Most MPs are also members of committees, which look at issues in detail, from government policy and new laws to wider topics like human rights.

Working in their constituency
MPs work in their constituency and hold regular advice 'surgery' in their office, where local residents can come along to discuss any matters that concern them.

MPs also attend functions in their community such as, a visit to schools and businesses and generally try to meet as many people as possible. This gives MPs more understanding and perspective into issues they may discuss when they go to Parliament.

MS CHI ONWURAH MP
Labour Party 2010 - Date

Chi Onwurah is a British Member of Parliament representing Newcastle upon Tyne Central and is also Shadow Minister for Culture & the Digital Economy.

From Jan 2013 - Sept 2015 Chi was Shadow Cabinet Office Minister leading on cyber security, social entrepreneurship, civil contingency, open government and transparency. From Oct 2010 – Jan 2013, Chi was Shadow Minister for Innovation, Science & Digital Infrastructure working closely with the Science and business community, with industry on Broadband issues, and on the Enterprise and Regulatory Reform Bill. Chi continues to encourage women in STEM.

From time to time, Chi has been engaged in local and international projects such as Chair of the All Party Parliamentary Group for Africa, APPG Adult Education, Founder and Chair and Parliamentary Internet, Communications and Technology Forum (Pictfor), Co-Chair

Prior to Chi's election to Parliament in May 2010 she worked as Head of Telecom's Technology at the UK regulator Ofcom focussing on the implications for competition and regulation of the services and technologies associated with Next Generation Networks.

Prior to Ofcom, Chi was a Partner in Hammatan Ventures, a US technology consultancy, developing the GSM markets in Nigeria and South Africa. Previously she was Director of Market Development with Teligent, a Global Wireless Local Loop operator and Director of Product Strategy at GTS. She has also worked for Cable & Wireless and Nortel as Engineer, Project and Product Manager in the UK and France

Chi is a Chartered Engineer with a BEng in Electrical Engineering from Imperial College London and an MBA from Manchester Business School. She was born in Wallsend and attended Kenton Comprehensive School in Newcastle, where she was elected the school's 'MP' in mock elections aged 17.

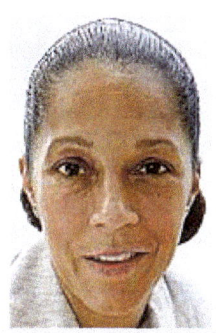

MRS HELEN GRANT MP
Conservative Party; 2010 to Date
Constituency: Maidstone & The Weald

Born in London to a single mum, Helen was brought up on a tough council estate in northern England for much of her early childhood. At school, she excelled at sport representing the County in Hockey, Tennis, Athletics, and Cross-Country, later becoming under-16 Judo Champion in the North of England and Southern Scotland.

Helen obtained a law degree at the University of Hull, attended the College of Law in Guildford, qualified as a solicitor in 1988 and became a Partner in 1992. In 1996, she set up her own firm specialising in the multiple challenges surrounding family breakdown, before becoming actively involved in politics in 2006.

Helen Grant was elected as Member of Parliament for the constituency of Maidstone & The Weald at the 2010 General Election, becoming the first Anglo-African female Conservative MP.

Helen is married and has two adult children.

Positions held in Parliament:
2013 – 2015   Minister for Sport and Tourism.
2012 – 2014 Minister for Women & Equalities
2012 – 2013   Minister for Justice
Boards and Committees affiliation:
2015 – 2016 Member of the International development select committee.
2010 – 2012 Member of the Justice select committee
2016 – Trustee of the Social Mobility Foundation.
She was appointed as Conservative Party's Vice Chair for Communities in January 2018.

KATE OSAMOR MP
Labour Party; May 2015 to Date

Kate Osamor is a Member of Parliament (MP) for Edmonton since May 2015. She was appointed Shadow Secretary of State for International Development in June 2016.

Kate Osamor was born to Nigerian parents and grew up in North London; Kate was educated at Creighton comprehensive school and read Third World Studies at the University of East London. After graduating, she then worked for 15 years in the NHS and was a GP practice manager before becoming an MP.

Kate is a community and trade union activist, and a trustee of a women's charity based in Edmonton Green.

Kate Osamor was appointed by the Labour leader, Jeremy Corbyn to the Official Opposition frontbench as Shadow Minister for Women and Equalities on 14 January 2016.

Kate was moved to the position of Shadow Secretary of State for International Development following Brexit on 27 June 2016.

CHUKA UMUNNA MP
Labour Party; May 2010 to Date

Chuka Umunna, Member of Parliament for Streatham was elected at the 2010 general election and was elected again in 2015 for the second term.

Chuka Umunna was born to a Nigerian father and English-Irish mother, Chuka grew up in Streatham and attended local schools. He studied Law at the University of Manchester and the University of Burgundy, followed by Nottingham Law School.

Following his education and further training at a City law firm, he specialised as a solicitor in employment law and acted for both employees and employers.

He was elected as a member of the Treasury Select Committee In June 2010 and in October 2010 he was appointed to serve as Parliamentary Private Secretary to Ed Miliband. In May 2011, Chuka was appointed as Shadow Secretary of State for Business, Innovation and Skills. He left this role in autumn 2015.

Chuka Umunna is the chair of All-Party Parliamentary Group (APPG) on Social Integration and a member of Home Affairs Select Committee.

Source: chuka.org.uk

FIONA ONASANYA MP
Labour Party; 2017 -

Fiona Onasanya was elected Member of Parliament for Peterborough in June 2017. She had previously represented Labour in Cambridgeshire County as a councillor for King's Hedges and held office from 2013 to 2017. During this time, she was spokesperson for *Children, Young People and Families, Group Whip* and Deputy Leader for the *Labour County Group*. A solicitor at DC Law in St Ives, Cambridgeshire, Fiona is also a Trustee member for the *East Hertfordshire YMCA*.

Having previously undertaken general Commercial Property work, Onasanya has significant experience in acting for Developers and Care Home Providers, dealing with their residential plot sales and setting up additional residential schemes/phases including the preparation of legal packs for onward plot sales, dealing with more straightforward disposals (and acquisitions in the event that pre-emption rights were exercised). Her specialties include Residential Development, Commercial & Residential Property.

For her, the journey into politics was an interesting one having started in Law, qualified as a Solicitor and had always planned to be a Solicitor. But it has since transpired that her love for legislation and the welfare of the community members would invariably lead her on to follow the path which now lies before her.

BIM AFOLAMI MP
Conservative Party; 2017 –
Bim Afolami, newly elected Conservative MP for Hitchin and Harpenden is originally from Crowthorne, an affluent village and rural parish in the Bracknell Forest district of Berkshire.

He attended Bishopsgate prep school, and Eton, later studying modern history at Oxford. He also trained as a lawyer.

The 31-year-old father of two is a school governor and has mentored teenagers. The son of an NHS consultant and a pharmacist, Bim is a supporter of charities which focus on helping people return to work. He contested Lewisham Deptford in the 2015 General Election, is a former Treasurer of the Bow Group and was Vice President of the Oxford Union in his university days.

He would later serve as a political adviser at the House of Commons and had previously worked for Howard Flight and George Osborne. He also had a stint in corporate law before moving on to finance as a senior executive at HSBC.

Described as an 'astute public speaker', Bim Afolami is a big sports fan and sportsman, supporting Northampton Saints and Arsenal FC.

Source: http://www.conservativehome.com/parliament/2017/05/exclusive-afolami-selected-as-conservative-candidate-for-hitchin-and-harpenden.html

KEMI BADENOCH MP
Conservative Party; 2017 -

Kemi Badenoch, the elected Member of Parliament for Saffron Walden, was born in Wimbledon into a large and loving family. Kemi grew up living in the United States and Nigeria, thus giving her a very global perspective on life.

She was previously a Conservative Party member of the London Assembly and the GLA Conservative's spokesman for the Economy, while also sitting on the Transport Committee and Policing and Crime Committee.

Before the Assembly, Kemi was a director at the *Spectator* Magazine and before that an associate director at *Coutts & Co*. She holds two degrees in engineering and law, from Sussex University and Birkbeck College respectively. She is currently a board member for the *Centre for the Study of British Politics and Public Life* and for nine years was a non-executive director for a London housing association.

Her other areas of interest include engineering and technology, social mobility and integration. She provides regular mentoring to women who wish to pursue careers in technology.

Kemi was recently a keynote speaker at *The Conservative Progress Brexit* conference where she explained her vision for a more united Britain outside of the EU. She has also spoken at the global *TedX* speaker series on addressing the poverty of ambition when it comes to ethnic minorities.

On the 2nd of May 2017, Kemi was selected as the Conservative parliamentary candidate for the Saffron Walden constituency and elected as a Member of Parliament (MP) at the June 8 UK general elections.

She was appointed as the Conservative Party's Vice Chair for Candidates in January 2018.

Reference: http://www.parliament.uk/mps-lords-and-offices/mps/

ROLE OF THE MAYORS/SPEAKERS

The office of Mayor continues to have a central part to play in modern councils and modern society. There are three vital roles for the Mayor in today's local authority and society:
- as a symbol of authority - robes, chains, etc. are indicators of this authority. The Mayor speaks for the whole Borough and gives identity to the Borough.
- as a symbol of an open society - any class, religion, etc.
- as an expression of social cohesion - acts as a link between many organisations.

Below are examples of the diverse activities of the Mayor/Speaker.

Diplomacy
As First Citizen, the Mayor has a diplomatic role and offers an official welcome to visitors to the Borough, hosting Civic Receptions and other functions. Mayor of the Borough speaks as such on behalf of the area and its community. Within the city boundaries only the monarch and in certain circumstances, the Lord Lieutenant of the borough, take precedence over the Mayor.

Promoting the Borough
The Mayor is involved in promoting the Borough, forging links with business and commerce, attending events organised by local and regional societies and professional organisations, and

attending official openings and presentations, opening of conferences and presiding over.

Close links exist between the Mayor and local community groups and a range of organisations such as schools, hospitals and residential homes.

Community/Charitable events
Mayor attends many functions in support of voluntary and charitable organisations as well as supporting many good causes throughout the borough. During Mayoral year, Mayor may have their own charity that they would like to support by raising funds and promoting the charity.

Religious events
In his or her year of office, the Mayor will attend a variety of religious services of all denominations. As part of these diverse duties, there are a number of regular annual events which each Mayor attends during his/her year of office.

Chairing council meetings
The primary function of Mayor is to chair the council meetings. The way in which the mayor chairs council meetings make a significant contribution to good governance. A well-run meeting that is inclusive and has high standards of governance relies on the mayor's style to being chair. Mayors should have a good knowledge of meeting procedures and their council's meetings local law.

Effective chairing also ensures that all councillors have the opportunity to be heard. While not every councillor can get his or her way on an issue, they are more likely to accept a decision if they feel that they have been included in the process.

The mayor should ensure that all councillors have had the opportunity to express their views, even if their proposals are defeated. Group facilitation concepts such as participation, communication, involvement, consensus, mutual respect and listening are all important in promoting the success of the councillor group.

Legal Duties
Parliamentary Elections: The Mayor is required to receive the writ for the holding of Parliamentary elections and sometimes act as Returning Officer.

Sealing of Documents
The Mayor is required to sign his or her name on legal documents involving the Council. The documents are normally presented to the Mayor for signature together with the Seal Register which must also be signed.

Citizenship
The Mayor also presides over citizenship ceremony for people who want to become British Citizen.

Source: London Government Directory: A guide to local government in London (2016). London Communications Agency.

- See more at
http://www.goodgovernance.org.au/roles-relationships/roles-in-local-government/mayor/#sthash.teiV2krz.dpuf
https://en.wikipedia.org/wiki/Lambeth_London_Borough_Council_elections

PAST AND CURRENT MAYORS/ SPEAKERS OF NIGERIAN HERITAGE

CLLR JANET ADEGOKE
Mayor of Hammersmith
1986-1987

CLLR ERELU LOLA AYONRINDE
Mayor of Wandsworth
1999/200 & 2004/2005

CLLR AFOLASADE BRIGHT
Speaker Hackney Borough
2006-2007

CLLR ROTIMI ADEBARI
Mayor of Portaoise
Town Council
(Republic of Ireland)
2007

Past And Current Mayors/ Speakers Of Nigerian Heritage

CLLR EMMANUEL OBASOHAN
Mayor of Barking & Dagenham
2008-2009

CLLR ANNA MBACHU
Mayor of Waltham Forest
2009-2010

CLLR TAYO SITU
Mayor of Southwark
2010-2011

CLLR SUSAN FAJANA-THOMAS
Speaker of Hackney
2011-2012

CLLR KATE ANOLUE
Mayor of Enfield
2012-2013

CLLR MICHAEL ADEYEYE
Mayor of Brent
2012 -2013

CLLR IRENE FASEYI
Mayor of Cheshire East
2013-2014

CLLR ADEDAMOLA AMINU
Mayor of Lambeth
2014-2015

CLLR MERCY UMEH
Mayor of Hammersmith & Fulham
2014-2017

CLLR OBAJIMI ADEFIRANYE
Chair of Council, Lewisham
2010 – Date

CLLR DONATUS ANYAWU
Mayor of Lambeth
2015-2016

CLLR SADE ETTI
Speaker of Hackney
2015-2016

CLLR PAT EKECHI
Mayor of Enfield
2015-2016

CLLR OLUGBENGA BABATOLA
Mayor of Greenwich
2016-2017

CLLR TUNDE OJETOLA
Mayor of Thurrock
2017-2018

CLLR YEMI OSHO
Mayor of Waltham Forest
2017-2018

CLLR SORAYA ADEJARE
*Speaker of Hackney
2017-2018*

Role of Councillors

Councillors are democratically elected to represent the people, and as thus they are accountable to the community in their local authority. They are the ultimate policy makers and carry out a number of strategic and corporate management functions.

Every service provided by a council is managed in their name by officers. All Councillors in their local authorities undertake many roles. Some of the roles are listed below.

- Speaking on behalf of the Council as a whole
- Public consultation and campaigning
- Policy formulation and making decisions, particularly major decisions affecting their local authority such as Housing, Licensing, Education, Social Services, Planning, Transport, Environment, setting Rent, Council Tax, Service Charge etc.
- Contribute to the good governance of the area and to actively encourage citizen involvement in decision making
- Attending meetings of the Council and its Committees etc
- Dealing with constituency issues/surgeries by responding to their enquiries and representations fairly and impartially.

- Attending political group meetings
- Attending public meetings and speaking as a community spokesperson
- Meetings with external agencies, private, public and voluntary sector groups
- Service and performance monitoring
- Acting as a chairperson/Spokesperson
- Acting as an ambassador on behalf of their local council both in a regional, national and international context
- Acting as a Group Leader/Deputy Leader of a political Group on the Council
- Being responsible as an employer for a large public sector organisation and maintain the highest standards of conduct and ethics.

BARKING & DAGENHAM BOROUGH

Borough Statistical Profile: Barking and Dagenham
Population   202,400
Ethnicity
White
White British   91,945   49.5%
White Irish   1,730   0.9%
White Gypsy or Irish Traveller   182   0.1%
White other   14,525   7.8%

Mixed
White & black Caribbean   2,669   1.4%
White & black African   2,128   1.1%
White & Asian   1,246   0.7%
Mixed others   1,835   1.0%

Asian or Asian British
Indian   7,436   4.0%
Pakistani   8,007   4.3%
Bangladeshi   7,701   4.1%
Asian other   5,135   2.8%

Black or Black British
Caribbean   5,227   2.8%
African   28,685   15.4%
Black other   3,228   1.7%

Arab   973   0.5%

Chinese or other
Chinese   1,315   0.7%
Other ethnic group   1,940   1.0%

Source: London Government Directory: A guide to local government in London (2016). London Communications Agency.

CLLR EMMANUEL OBASOHAN

Labour; Becontree Ward; 2006 - 2014
Mayor; 2008 - 2009

He represented *Becontree Ward* for Labour from 2006 to 2014. Cllr Obasohan was the Mayor for the year 2008/2009

CLLR JAMES OGUNGBOSE

Labour Party; 2010 - Date

Cllr James Ogungbose was the cabinet member for central services and is a councillor for the *Becontree Ward*. His committee appointments include *Assembly, Ceremonial Council, Living & Working Select Committee, Pensions Panel and the Public Accounts & Audit Select Committee*. Cllr Ogungbose is also appointed to serve (outside) on the *Barking & Dagenham Citizens' Advice Bureau*

COUNCILLOR AFOLASADE BRIGHT

2002 – 2010 (Hackney); 2014 – Date (Barking & Dagenham)

Afolasade Bright has been involved in British politics for over 18 years as a Mayor and Councillor in two different Boroughs. She became Civic Mayor of Hackney in 2006, the first African and certainly the first Nigerian in the borough to hold the office, and that of deputy Mayor respectfully. Prior to becoming Mayor she was elected as the Chair of Hackney Labour Group and Director of Hackney Homes. Amongst many commitments, in Hackney she chaired meetings of the full council, served as School Governor and Honorary President of Age Concern UK. In Barking and Dagenham Cllr Bright is the Women and Gender Equalities champion and socio-political campaigner for women's rights, trustee of many local organisations and First Cabinet Member for Equalities and Cohesion. She is a member of the prestigious London Mayor's and London Labour Mayor's Associations.

A Fellow of the Chartered Institute of Personnel and Development, Cllr Bright holds an LLB (Hons) and Masters in Employment and Human Resources Management. She worked in local authority for over 18 years in various senior management roles before leaving to start an Education/HR consultancy, *Bright Futurez* with her husband Pastor Gbolahan Bright MBE. Cllr Bright is a co-Pastor of the Redeemed Christian Church of God - The Master's Sanctuary and a sought after speaker at corporate and church conferences and events.

She is the Founder and President of *The Sapphirez* women's organisation and The Pennu Charity for older people. She supports and fundraises for many nominated charities including Age Concern UK, St Joseph's Hospice Hackney, Richards House Children's Charity and The Bright Free Maths Project. She founded Extraordinaire, a project geared to mentoring young women and girls through her Political and Leadership Mentoring Academy, training and empowering young people to take up leadership roles in the community. There are currently over 100 young people benefitting from this project.

She has received several awards both in the UK and abroad and was voted as "Councillor of The Year 2006" at the Gathering of Africa's Best - GAB Awards UK.

Cllr Sade Bright is an award winning Author of a book entitled, 'Dream Big: Stretch Your Boundaries'. The book was carefully crafted to uplift and support the belief that you can achieve all you had considered impossible. "It will allow you - the reader the strength to define who you wish to be and equip you with the required tools to live the life of your dreams". She recently released another book entitled: "Mastering English

Language – Reinforcing Reading & Writing Skills – Key Stage 2". She is happily married with three children.

CLLR ADEGBOYEGA OLUWOLE

Labour Party; Mayesbrook Ward;
2014 - Date

Cllr Oluwole's Committee appointments included: Assembly, Ceremonial Council, Children's Services Select Committee, Licensing & Regulatory Board, Licensing Sub-Committee, Personnel Board & Public Accounts & Audit Select Committee. His appointments to outside bodies are in the *Admissions Forum, Elevate Strategic Partner Board, Governing Body - The Adult College of Barking and Dagenham* and the *OFSTED Report Panel.*

CLLR SANCHIA ALASIA

Barking & Dagenham (by Marriage)
Labour Party; Alibon Ward; 2010 - date

Sanchia Alasia is a Labour Councillor for Alibon Ward. An award winning specialist in equality diversity and Human Resource she joined the Council in 2010, and held a number of positions - School Governor, chair of the health and adult services scrutiny committee and currently as chair of DCB, she has successfully steered the committee through some complex planning applications. She has been a member of DCB for the past 5 years, taking decisions on major developments. Cllr Alasia possess an excellent knowledge in planning law and experience.

Sanchia was one of the Labour Party candidates for the European Elections in 2015 in the London region. With a BSc in Politics and Sociology and an MSc in Politics, Policy and Government, she is well read.

Sanchia is a well-sought-after speaker and has spoken at the *World Diversity Leadership Summit* and the *European Diversity Business Congress* over the last couple of years. We've also shared the same platform as guest speakers on numerous occasions.

As well as being an active member of the Labour Party, Cllr Alasia is an active member of the *Fabian Society*, *Co-op Party*, *Christian Socialist Movement*, *BAME Labour* and her trade union, *UNISON*.

It is interesting to note that in 2010 when she was first elected, she became the youngest woman on the Council and with her colleagues achieved over a 7% Labour swing from the BNP as they had reached out to a wider community. Sanchia won the Local Government Personality of the year at the *Dods Women in Public Life Awards*. She was also a winner at the *Grassroots Diplomats Awards* in the policy driver category for her work in equality and diversity.

BEXLEY BOROUGH

Population	239,865	
Ethnicity		
White		
White British	179,250	77.3%
White Irish	2,596	1.1%
White Gypsy or Irish Traveller	624	0.3%
White other	7,492	3.2%
Mixed		
White & black Caribbean	1,676	0.7%
White & black African	983	0.4%
White & Asian	1,369	0.6%
Mixed others	1,367	0.6%
Asian or Asian British		
Indian	7,047	3.0%
Pakistani	730	0.3%
Bangladeshi	777	0.3%
Asian other	4,175	1.8%
Black or Black British		
Caribbean	2,381	1.0%
African	15,952	6.9%
Black other	1,291	0.6%
Arab	303	0.1%
Chinese or other		
Chinese	2514	1.1%
Other ethnic group	1470	0.6%

Source: London Government Directory: A guide to local government in London (2016). London Communications Agency.

CLLR ENDY EZENWATA
Labour Party; Thames East Ward;
2014 - Date

Councillor Ndubuisi Endy Ezenwata was born in Udo, Ezinihitte Mbaise in the Imo State of Nigeria to the late Rev and Mrs Rowland Ezenwata over 36years ago.

The 3rd child in a family of 5, he was educated at Government College Umuahia, IMT Enugu and Bexley College London. Cllr Ezenwata is currently studying part-time for a Law degree with the Open University London.

He played professional football briefly with *Gombe United* in Nigeria before travelling abroad to Malta in 1998 to pursue a footballing career. His football career ended early as a result of a recurring knee injury in 2001 when he then moved to the UK. He went on to work as a Department Manager with *Asda Distribution* and also worked with *Tesco Deliveries* before venturing into local politics in 2010 when he was elected as the 1st Nigerian to serve as a Councillor in the London Borough of Bexley in 2014.

Endy enjoys travelling, playing football, discovering other cultures, volunteering for charity work, advocating for the needy, and praising and worshipping God. He lives with his wife and four children (2 boys and two girls). In his spare time, he does a lot of community work, organising projects, peer mentoring and he is also a motivational speaker.

Position held in council included *Shadow Cabinet Member for Environment & Public Realm* and as Committee member of *Overview Scrutiny*.

He is also School Governor at *Northwood Primary School*, a volunteer football coach at *All Stars U8 Thamesmead*, President of *Ezinihitte Mbaise Community UK Union*, Chairman of *Udo Nwere Madu Foundation* (a Nigerian NGO) and Chairman of *Udo Peoples Assembly UK & Ireland*.

CLLR MABEL OGUNDAYO
Labour Party; Thamesmead East Ward; 2014 - date

Mabel Ogundayo was elected in 2014 under the platform of Labour Party for London Borough of Bexley. She is the Deputy Leader of *Bexley Labour Group*, Shadow Cabinet Member for Children's Services, Labour Lead on *People's Overview and Scrutiny*.

Mabel also serves on the *Bexley Standing Advisory Council on Religious Education* (SACRE) (Substitute); Council - *Extraordinary Council Meeting*; *General Purposes Committee* (Substitute); *Licensing Committee*; *People Overview and Scrutiny Committee*; *Resources Overview and Scrutiny Committee* (Substitute) and *Top Management Review Panel*.

BRENT BOROUGH

Population	322,400	
Ethnicity		
White		
White British	55,887	18%
White Irish	12,320	4.0%
White Gypsy or Irish Traveller	320	0.1%
White other	44,353	14.3%
Mixed		
White & black Caribbean	4,291	1.4%
White & black African	2,820	0.9%
White & Asian	3,642	1.2%
Mixed others	5,022	1.6%
Asian or Asian British		
Indian	58,017	18.6%
Pakistani	14,381	4.6%
Bangladeshi	1,749	0.6%
Asian other	28,589	9.2%
Black or Black British		
Caribbean	23,723	7.6%
African	24,391	7.8%
Black other	10,518	3.4%
Arab	11,430	3.7%
Chinese or other		
Chinese	3,250	1.0%
Other ethnic group	6,512	2.1%

Source: London Government Directory: A guide to local government in London (2016). London Communications Agency.

CLLR MICHAEL ADEYEYE BSC (HONS), CMIOSH, MIIRSM

Labour Party; Queen's Pak Ward; 2010 -2014
Mayor; 2012 - 2013

Mayor of the London Borough of Brent (2012-2013). He is a retired health and safety practitioner. Married with four grown up children, he has lived in the London Borough of Brent for many years. He is an active politician, an environmentalist and champion of fair-trading.

His background is in Safety and Health Management. He is a Chartered Member of the Institution of Occupational Safety and Health (IOSH) as well as the International Institute of Safety Management (IIRSM).

He is a community activist who has been involved with various voluntary and statutory organisations in Brent and beyond. He has a strong commitment to the Borough and its people and thoroughly enjoys being a part of the community, taking part in a variety of charitable works and community events.

As a Councillor, he served on Planning and Health select Committees. He was Chair of Disability Forum; Executive member of Queens Park Consultative Forum and London Road Safety Council.

Hobbies include gardening, photography, travelling, world affairs and mixing with people from different backgrounds and cultures.

CLLR TAYO OLADAPO

Labour Party; Kilburn Ward; 2010 – 2016

Councillor Tayo Oladapo represented the Kilburn Ward since his election in 2010, and was always keen to improve the lives of his constituents. He had served on various committees including the *Alcohol & Entertainment Licensing Committee* from 2010 to 2013, the *Children & Families Overview and Scrutiny Committee* until 2011 and later, the *Scrutiny Committee* from 2014 to 15.

Cllr Oladapo passed away on 29th January 2016 after a period of illness.

CLLR ERNEST NNAAMA EZEAJUGHI

Labour Party; Stonebridge Ward; 2014 - Date

Born in 1970 and a graduate of Medical Microbiology, Cllr Ezeajughi also has a post graduate degree in Environmental Health Management from the prestigious Kings College London (KCL).

In 2004, he relocated to the United Kingdom where he joined the Labour Party the same year considering his admiration for politics, a platform he would use to serve humanity and a way of giving back to his community.

Ten years later, he contested the election as a councillor in Stonebridge Ward, London Borough of Brent, on the Labour Party platform. After being elected as a councillor in May 2014, he convened all Nigerians residing and working in Brent to form "Brent Nigerian Community" which was a pioneering effort, and now the Nigerian Independence celebrations and other Nigerian events now hold yearly since that time.

Cllr Ezeajughi has served in several committees in Brent Council since his election including the *Planning Committee*. He is happily married with four children.

CLLR AISHA ENIOLA
Labour Party; Harlesden Ward; 2014 – Date

Aisha Eniola made history in 2014 when she won an election to the Brent Council as a 19-year-old final year Mass Communications student in a London University. Aisha is daughter of former Welsh Harp Councillor, Francis Eniola and represents Harlesden Ward. From time to time she has been engaged in local and international projects. Youth projects, homeless.

Her Committee appointments included the *Alcohol & Entertainment Licensing Committee* and *Council*.

CLLR BENJAMIN OLUKAYODE OGUNRO

Labour Party; Kilburn Ward; 2010 - 2014

Cllr Benjamin Olukayode Ogunro was born in Lagos and attended CMS Grammar School, the oldest secondary school in Lagos. He worked at Lagos General Hospital and was awarded a study leave to pursue professional qualification at the Bristol Royal Infirmary School of Radiography where he qualified with distinction as a Radiographer. He then moved to London when he got a job as a Senior Radiographer at Kings College Hospital at Camberwell in London.

Cllr Ogunro was appointed as the Chief Radiographer in Saudi Arabia for three years. He had joined the Labour Party in 1970 and became a Labour Councillor for Kilburn Ward at Brent Council for 4years. Because of his medical background, he was elected the Chairman of the Medical Scrutiny Committee for one year. He decided to leave the scene for younger members in 2014.

His political life has not changed though: he remains a staunch member of the Labour Party. Benjamin believes in social interaction and so as a Lagosian, he became a life member of the Island Club and Yoruba Tennis Club of Lagos where he can interact with old school mates and at the same time, making new friends.

ENFIELD BOROUGH

Population	331,500	
Ethnicity		
White		
White British	126,450	40.5%
White Irish	6,899	2.2%
White Gypsy or Irish Traveller	344	0.1%
White other	56,947	18.2%
Mixed		
White & black Caribbean	4,852	1.6%
White & black African	2,384	0.8%
White & Asian	4,189	1.3%
Mixed others	5,758	1.8%
Asian or Asian British		
Indian	11,648	3.7%
Pakistani	2,594	0.8%
Bangladeshi	5,599	1.8%
Asian other	12,464	4.0%
Black or Black British		
Caribbean	17,334	5.5%
African	28,222	9.0%
Black other	8,131	2.6%
Arab	1,930	0.6%
Chinese or other		
Chinese	2,588	0.8%
Other ethnic group	14,133	4.5%

Source: London Government Directory: A guide to local government in London (2016). London Communications Agency.

CLLR KATE NDIDI ANOLUE

Labour Party; Upper Edmonton Ward;
2002 – 2014
Deputy Mayor; 2011 – 2012
Mayor; 2012 - 2013

Elected as a Councillor for Upper Edmonton Ward in 2002-2014, Cllr Kate Anolue brings to public service a wide array of experience in both the public and the organised private sectors.

With over thirty years working within the London community as a midwife, Kate has a wealth of knowledge and experience in many of the social and health issues that are prevalent in communities. Coupled with over ten years' experience in politics which included Deputy Mayor (2011/2012) and Mayor of the London Borough of Enfield for 2012/2013, Kate has consolidated all her experience so as to help champion community causes like health, crime and safety, children and young people issues, single parents and other disadvantaged groups. She understands and works for the needs of the diverse community in Enfield, and represents them by advocating on their behalf.

Her public service portfolio in the borough includes: *Chair of Housing Scrutiny* (2010/11), *Member of Planning Committee* (May 2010 to 2014), *Member of the Enfield Scrutiny Commission* (elected September 2009), *Chair of Labour Group* (May 2009 to May 2011), *WOMEN OFFICER for Edmonton Constituency* (May 2005 to May 2008) and Chair, *Health Scrutiny* (May 2003 to May 2005).

Such dedication as Cllr Anolue has demonstrated hardly goes without due recognition. She has been honoured by the community in so many ways. Some of her awards included the

Nigerian Watch newspaper (UK) *Woman of the Year 2014*; the *Black Entertainment Film Fashion Television & Arts* (*BEFFTA*) *Award for Leadership* awarded in October 2014 and the following month, the *Nigeria National Communities* (*NNC*) London *Award for Leadership*.

She has previously been honoured by the organisers of one of UK's longest running honours presentation bodies, the *Gathering of African Best* (*GAB Awards*) in December 2013.

In June 2014, Cllr Anolue was one of the 100 recipients of the *Nigerian Centenary Awards* organised in the United Kingdom to mark the Nigerian centenary celebration.

Cllr Kate Anolue is the Chief Executive of *TenderCare Health Initiative*; an NGO set up to become both a support/mentoring organisation for teenage pregnant girls particularly those under 16. The initiative also supports young fathers, fathers-to-be, vulnerable and lonely women. Since 2013 till date, Kate serves as the

CEO, *Forum for African, African Caribbean & Asian Women in Politics* (FAWP). She is school governor of two schools, *Raynham* and *Wilbury Primary Schools* and a trustee member of *Hanlon Centre*, *Enfield Women Centre* and *Enfield Law Centre* for over five years until it became non-functional.

On April 16th, 2007, Anolue was conferred with the *Honorary Freedom of the London Borough of Enfield*. This is the highest honour conferred on an individual in recognition of the long and valuable service to the community and outstanding contribution to the voluntary sector in the borough.

A community advocate and people's champion, she was conferred with the Chieftaincy title – "*Ada Jere Mba Turu Ugo*" in December 2008. The title translates "*Our daughter that went to foreign land and brought us glory*".

Cllr Anolue has degrees from the North Middlesex University Hospital and the University of North London. She is currently matron of the *Congress of Igbo Leaders UK & Ireland*, President of *Igbo Catholic Community UK & Ireland* and the *Nigerian Catholic Community*, St. Edmunds, Edmonton.

Kate Anolue hold the membership of the prestigious *International Women of Power* (*IWOP*).

CLLR. (MS) NNEKA KEAZOR
Labour Party; Enfield Lock Ward;
2010 - Date

Cllr (Ms) Nneka Keazor, elected in 2010 on a platform of the Labour Party is a serving councillor of the council at Enfiled. Ms Keazor currently holds the position of the Chair of *Overview & Scrutiny Committee* and a serving member of the *Enfield B*. Her community engagement has also seen her serving in various capacities on the *Enfield Lock Ward Forum, Extraordinary Council* and the *Speech & Language Therapy Scrutiny Workstream*.

Her engagements outside of Council include sitting membership of the *Enfield Racial Equality Council*. Nneka is also involved in a youth programme under the London Borough of Haringey and several local projects in her Ward, primarily Enfield Lock - funded through the *Enfield Resident Priority Fund* and the *Community First Grant*

Cllr. Keazor is actively involved in the BAME Labour Party, thus ensuring visible representation of ethnic minority candidates and membership on all panels and community engagement forums.

She holds the responsibility for coordinating Nigerian residents in Enfield and organising a celebratory event in August 2014 in partnership with other Nigerian councillors in Enfield, with *BEN Television* promoting and screening the event. This project was set to ensure Diaspora community building.

Nneka is a Trustee of a charity organisation, *Community Gateway Project*, responsible for providing extra curriculum activities for youth in the local area. Versatile and highly motivated, Cllr Keazor is a senior manager with a wealth of professional and soft skills experience acquired across a wide range of challenging roles with over 20 years post graduation experience in Business Processes and Project Management within the public service sector.

Among her other qualifications are *BSc Biochemistry*, *MSc Business Information Technology*, *LLB* and *PGD Legal Practice*. She remains passionate about and is proudly committed to children's services and advocating for the less privileged and the ethnic minority community at large. Hers is a lifetime of commitment to working at the grassroots so as to ensuring that all the residents have access to improved and better services.

CLLR OZZIE UZOANYA
Labour Party; Enfield Lock Ward;
2010-2017

Cllr. Ozzie Uzoanya Uzodike was elected in 2010 on the platform of the Labour Party and is still serving till date. Ozzie is *Associate Cabinet Member for Enfield North* and holds committee appointments serving on the *Conservation Advisory Group*, *Enfield Lock Ward Forum* and the *Extraordinary Council*.

He also serves a member of the *Belling Educational Foundation*. An astutely committed member with experience in strategic development, policy and planning, Cllr. Uzoanya is involved in an assembly, *Nigerians in Enfield*, a community group which seeks to empower people of Nigerian descent thereby enabling them to play a greater role in the civic life of the borough.

CHIEF COUNCILLOR PATRICIA CHINYERE NMAKU EKECHI (Nee ANAH)

Councillor Patricia Ekechi joined the Labour Party in 1997. She was first elected a Councillor in 2010 representing Haselbury Ward, Edmonton in the London Borough of Enfield.

She served as a School Governor for eight years in one of the borough's schools. She is a member in many residential community organisations and housing associations.

She was a Board Member with one of the local Housing Associations, St Pancras Housing Association (now Origin) for several years in late 1990s and early 2000.

Councillor Patricia Ekechi has three grown children, two sons and a daughter, all university graduates, and in good jobs. Her daughter is a Consultant at the Queen Charlotte Hospital in London. Councillor Patricia Ekechi also has a five year old grandson.

She was the Edmonton Branch CLP Black and Ethnic Minority's Officer for four years, the Edmonton South Branch Vice Chair for two years and the CLP Disability Office for a year.

She was the Labour Party Councillors' Women's Officer for two years, the Labour Party Councillors' Deputy Whip. She was re-elected in 2014 representing the Upper Edmonton Ward.

In June 2014 – May 2015 she was appointed the Enfield Borough's Deputy Mayor and in May 2015 – May 2016, Councillor Patricia Ekechi was elected the second Nigerian woman (and the first Ihiagwa, Owerri, Imo State, Nigerian woman) Mayor in Enfield. The First Citizen of the London Borough of Enfield.

She visited and supported a number of charities both locally and internationally. She raised a lot of funds which was distributed to her chosen charity Dementia and other charities such as the Blind community, deaf and dumb, International children voices, local care homes, and disabled community to name but few. She still engages herself in voluntary works in the community.

Councillor Patricia Ekechi has received numerous Awards from various organisations locally and outside the borough. She is still the Enfield Labour Group's Deputy Whip and recently appointed the Group's Vice Chair. She has a BSc Degrees in Social Sciences at the South Bank University.

Councillor Patricia Ekechi was made Chief, with title of *EZI ADA JERE MBA TURU UGO ONE OF IHIAGWA* in her home town in Ihiagwa, Owerri, Imo State, Nigeria in December 2010 for her hard works, supports and high achievements at home and abroad.

GREENWICH BOROUGH

Population   269,000

Ethnicity
White
White British   133,130   52.3%
White Irish   4,291   1.7%
White Gypsy or Irish Traveller   430   0.2%
White other   21,151   8.3%

Mixed
White & black Caribbean   4,011   1.6%
White & black African   2,699   1.1%
White & Asian   2,361   0.9%
Mixed others   3,203   1.3%

Asian or Asian British
Indian   7,836   3.1%
Pakistani   2,594   1.0%
Bangladeshi   1,645   0.6%
Asian other   12,758   5.0%

Black or Black British
Caribbean   8,051   3.2%
African   35,164   13.8%
Black other   5,440   2.1%

Arab   1,069   0.4%

Chinese or other
Chinese   5,061   2.0%
Other ethnic group   3,663   1.4%

Source: London Government Directory: A guide to local government in London (2016). London Communications Agency.

CLLR OLUGBENGA BABATOLA

Labour Party; Thamesmead Moorings Ward; 2014 - Date

Cllr Olugbenga Babatola has been a member of the Labour Party for over a decade and became more active in 2009. Since then he has held many positions within the ward and constituency including *Ward Secretary and Organiser*, CLP Organiser, *Member of the Local Campaign Forum* and presently the Vice Chair of the constituency.

In 2014, Olu Babatola was elected as a Councillor representing Thamesmead Moorings Ward. He was subsequently elected Deputy Mayor in 2015 and is honoured to be elected as Mayor of Royal Greenwich for 2016/17. He is also a School Governor at *Discovery Primary School*, Thamesmead and Chair of the Business Committee within the school.

He completed a Postgraduate Diploma in Management Studies at the Greenwich School of Management and became an Associate Member of the Association of Business Executives (AMABE). Alongside his academic work, he has worked in the retail industry and currently works as a Deputy Store Manager with a major retailer. Olu enjoyed athletics at school, in particular, long distance races, High Jump and Javelin. He was a keen footballer in his younger days.

CLLR TONIA ASHIKODI (MS)

Labour; Glyndon Ward; 2015 – Date

Councillor Tonia Ashikodi is a community-oriented, social entrepreneur political activist with a deep passion and expertise in business and communities. Her committee affiliations included *Housing & Anti-Poverty Scrutiny Panel* and *Community Safety & Environmental Scrutiny Panel*. Cllr Ashikodi has as appointments to outside bodies the *Overview & Scrutiny Joint Health Committee*, *Woolwich & District YMCA* and the *Woolwich & Plumstead Relief in Sickness Fund*. From time to time, she has also been engaged in other local and international projects.

A graduate of Kent Business School at the University of Kent, Canterbury Ms Ashikodi is deeply passionate about helping people from different backgrounds. Having had professional roles at *PricewaterhouseCoopers* and *Societe Generale*, she had ventured into social enterprise, an area where she runs the *Mumtrepreneur Club*, the club helps women who are at a disadvantage to build themselves whilst raising their children. She also serves as a director for the *F.E.E.D Project UK*, a charity organisation with a focus on helping disadvantaged people within local communities.

A devoted wife and mother of 3, Cllr Ashikodi envisions her role as that of making a change within her locality whilst creating lasting and positive impacts in the lives of people within and the UK at large.

HACKNEY BOROUGH

Population   262,800

Ethnicity
White
White British	89,030	36.2%
White Irish	5,216	2.1%
White Gypsy or Irish Traveller	474	0.2%
White other	39,897	16.2%

Mixed
White & black Caribbean	4,989	2.0%
White & black African	2,866	1.2%
White & Asian	3,020	1.2%
Mixed others	4,994	2.0%

Asian or Asian British
Indian	7,599	3.1%
Pakistani	1,905	0.8%
Bangladeshi	6,180	2.5%
Asian other	6,747	2.7%

Black or Black British
Caribbean	19,168	7.8%
African	27,976	11.4%
Black other	9,714	3.9%

Arab   1,721   0.7%

Chinese or other
Chinese	3,436	1.4%
Other ethnic group	11,338	4.6%

Source: London Government Directory: A guide to local government in London (2016). London Communications Agency.

CLLR SUSAN FAJANA-THOMAS

Labour Party; Stoke Newington Ward;
2010 – Date
Mayor (Speaker); 2011/2012

Cllr. Susan Fajana-Thomas, a Nigerian-British socio-political campaigner, is a Labour Party Councillor in the London Borough of Hackney and the former Mayor of Hackney. She is fondly referred to on the borough as 'Speaker'.

Since she was first elected, Susan has also served as Vice Chair, *Corporate Committee* and member of the *Planning Sub-Committee* and the *Stoke Newington Ward Forum*. Susan's appointments to outside bodies included serving on the *Abney Park Cemetery Trust* and the *East London NHS Foundation Trust* (Stoke Newington Ward). She has also served on the *Hackney Homes Board*, *Industrial Dwellings Society* and the *London Housing Consortium* (Stoke Newington Central Ward)

Educated at the *University of Ife* (now *Obafemi Awolowo University*) and *London School of Journalism*, she was a broadcaster with the *Nigerian Television Authority* (NTA) before relocating to the United Kingdom (UK). Since moving to North London over two decades ago, she has dedicated herself to contributing and having a positive impact in her local community as well as within the larger Nigerian and broader

African communities. Her campaigning priorities include housing, equality, women's rights and welfare of children.

Susan Fajana-Thomas is a recipient of numerous awards and recognitions from around the globe. She is one of the 100 Outstanding Nigerian-British recognised for their excellent contributions to the UK society over the last 100 years at the *Nigerian Centenary Celebrations* in the United Kingdom. She is also a *BEFFTA Community Leadership Award* recipient.

Cllr. Fajana-Thomas is a school governor at *Grasmere School* and has served in a variety of public offices with pride and distinction. She currently serves on the Board of Directors of seven organisations, including *London Housing Consortium*, *Industrial Dwelling Society*, *Finsbury Park Trust*, *Abney Park Cemetery Trust* and the *Nigerian Women in Diaspora Leadership Forum* (NWIDLF).

CLLR MICHAEL JONES
Labour Party; 2010 – 2014

Cllr Michael Jones, elected in May 2010 served until May 2014 on the platform of the Labour Party. He was Vice Chair of *Children and Young People* and had served on the Licensing Committee. Michael is a committed grassroots activist who proudly proclaims both his Nigerian parentage and dual (Nigerian-British) nationality.

The Hackney-born and raised councillor studied at the University of Goldsmiths and obtained a BSc (Hons) in *Applied Social Science and Youth Community Development* in 2008. Michael currently works for an organisation called *Cityzen* as a freelance facilitator, Youth Committee Coordinator and Youth Worker.

Born to a close-knit family with three brothers and a sister, he has been involved in volunteering since he was fifteen, doing youth participation work with local youth clubs. This has thus seen him developed to a more organised and tireless community activist.

At the local level, Michael has served on the *Local New Deal for Community* as an adult Board of Trustees member representing young people, a position he actively held from 2003 to 2006. He was also a member of the *Hackney Youth Parliament* from its inception in 2002 up till 2006.

Cllr. Michael Jones was the pioneer member elected from Hackney to sit in the *United Kingdom Youth Parliament* as a *Member of Youth Parliament* (MYP) from 2003 to 2005.

CLLR SADE ETTI
Labour Party; 2014 – Date
Speaker; 2015/2016

Cllr Sade Etti was born in Nigeria and is the mother of four lovely children. She moved to Hackney Borough in the United Kingdom in 2004 where she has lived with her family for more than ten years. She was elected to the Hackney Council in 2014.

Cllr Etti started her humanitarian journey as a member of the *Rotaract Club of Apata Ganga* (Ibadan, Oyo State of Nigeria) aged 17, helping the elderly and young, both within Ibadan and outside the state. She attended training for this purpose and contributed to the satellite charter of the *Rotaract Club of The Polytechnic Ibadan*, Esa Oke Satellite Campus. She maintains that the values of the Rotaract Club have been her watchword in the political terrain and this led to her advocating for people wherever she goes. She was also heavily immersed in student wellbeing and politics within the school campus, as she went on to become the Assistant Secretary and eventually Treasurer of the Students Union.

Councillor Etti joined the Labour Party in 2006 after the birth of her twins who were born prematurely at Homerton Hospital. The care and support she received from the community prompted her to join the party in a bid to give back. She chose to be a member of the Labour Party because the values and missions of the Party aligned with her personal principles and those of other political parties she had belonged to in the past in Nigeria. She became an active and enthusiastic member, supporter and proponent of the Labour Party.

She participated in campaigns, leafleting, stalls and various other activities for the party, became the Chair and Secretary of her ward, after that Women Affairs Officer for the constituency and represented the constituency at the Labour Party Conference. All these experiences led her to put herself forward for the position of a councillor. She was elected in 2014 as the council's newest member.

She became the Deputy Speaker in 2014 /2015, Speaker London Borough of Hackney 2015 to 2016 and is currently Chair of *Hackney Faith Network Forum* working together with all faith leaders in the borough. Cllr Etti is also Chair, *Community Safety* and *Social Inclusion Scrutiny Commission*.

Aside from her various roles within Hackney politics and beyond, Sade has also been involved in *Tenants Residents Association*, volunteered for a food bank and contributed to the food bank satellite section in *The Redeemed Evangelical Mission* (TREM) *Church* and also sits on the board of various organisations.

CLLR SORAYA ADEJARE

Labour Party; Dalston Ward; 2010 – Date
Deputy Mayor, 2016-2017; Mayor, 2017-2018

Cllr Soraya Adejare is the elected councillor representing the Dalston ward on the platform of the Labour Party.

Soraya grew up in Hackney and went to Woodberry Down School. She is an active resident representative for her estate and attends her local Community Advisory Panel meetings to make sure residents' concerns about crime and anti-social behaviour are raised. Soraya is also a member of Homerton NHS Trust.

Soraya works in local government and has covered a range of policy areas including learning disabilities, regeneration and governance services.

Soraya's priorities include ensuring that all residents are represented and can contribute to the discussion taking place as Dalston continues to change. She is particularly interested in planning, licensing, environmental enhancement, increasing affordable housing and provision for young people.

She was elected Speaker of Hackney Borough on 24th May 2017 to oversee events and activities for the year following. Cllr Adejare has previously served as the Deputy Speaker for the 2016/17 parliamentary year.

(Source: Dalston-Hackney Labour Party website)

CLLR KAM ADAMS

Labour Party; Hoxton East & Shoreditch; 2014 -Date

Cllr Adams was elected in 2014. He is the Labour Group Assistant Whip. Cllr Adams serves on the following committees; he is a member of *Living in Hackney Scrutiny Commission*, *Pensions Committee*, and *Standing Advisory Council for Religious Education* (SACRE).

He has BSc, Pg (Econ), MSc Econometrics, PRINCE2 Project Management, CCNA, CCNP (CISCO Networking). Lecturer in Economics, Business Studies and ICT.

HAMMERSMITH & FULHAM BOROUGH

Population 180,000

Ethnicity
White
White British	81,989	44.9%
White Irish	6,321	3.5%
White Gypsy or Irish Traveller	217	0.1%
White other	35,695	19.6%

Mixed
White & black Caribbean	2,769	1.5%
White & black African	1,495	0.8%
White & Asian	2,649	1.5%
Mixed others	3,131	1.7%

Asian or Asian British
Indian	3,451	1.9%
Pakistani	1,612	0.9%
Bangladeshi	1,056	0.6%
Asian other	7,376	4.0%

Black or Black British
Caribbean	7,111	3.9%
African	10,552	5.8%
Black other	3,842	2.1%

Arab 5,228 2.9%

Chinese or other
Chinese	3,140	1.7%
Other ethnic group	4,859	2.7%

Source: London Government Directory: A guide to local government in London (2016). London Communications Agency.

CLLR MERCY UMEH

Labour Party; Shepherds Bush Green Ward (2002 – 2014 – Date)
Deputy Mayor; 2003 – 2006;
Mayor; 2016/2017

The Worshipful the Mayor of the London Borough of Hammersmith & Fulham Councillor Mercy Umeh was re-elected to serve as Mayor on 18 May 2016 and previously served as Deputy Mayor from 2003 to 2006. She was first elected in 2002.

CLLR MRS. JANET ADEGOKE

Labour Councillor - 1986
Mayor (1987 – 1st Oct 1987)

Janet Olufunmilayo Adegoke came to England to study nursing when she was nineteen. She was born in West Africa in the Nigerian city of Ibadan. She campaigned strongly to unite Black and white communities as the secretary of the *Emlyn Gardens Tenants' Association*. Only two years after becoming a councillor, she was elected Mayor of Hammersmith and Fulham.

Janet Adegoke will go down in history, not only as a former mayor of Hammersmith and Fulham but also as the first Black woman in London to be made a Mayor. On completion of her nursing studies, she became involved in community work and was especially concerned with the issue of improved housing and living conditions. She was a popular local figure and gained a reputation as a tireless worker for the community. Janet Adegoke became well known as Secretary of the *Emlyn Gardens Tenants' Association*, a role she held for 12 years before joining the council. She was elected a councillor for the *Starch Green Ward* in 1986 and became Mayor of Hammersmith and Fulham in May 1987. Janet Adegoke was a co-founder of *Hammersmith African Link*, an organisation formed to support her fellow Africans in the borough. Equally, she is remembered as a moderate who worked hard to unite black and white communities. Alongside her dedicated work for the community, she had a full-time job and, as a single parent brought up three children. Sadly, Janet Adegoke died of cancer in October 1987, but she continued to carry out her official duties and engagements until a week before her death, aged 45. The new *Janet Adegoke Swimming Pool* in White City was opened in March 2006. The old leisure centre knocked down in 2003, had been named as a tribute to Janet Adegoke and the new pool keeps her name.

HARINGEY BOROUGH

Population	269,600	
Ethnicity		
White		
White British	88,424	34.7%
White Irish	6,997	2.7%
White Gypsy or Irish Traveller	370	0.1%
White other	58,552	23.0%
Mixed		
White & black Caribbean	4,856	1.9%
White & black African	2,609	1.0%
White & Asian	3,738	1.5%
Mixed others	5,345	1.2%
Asian or Asian British		
Indian	5,945	2.3%
Pakistani	1,920	0.8%
Bangladeshi	4,417	1.7%
Asian other	8,124	3.2%
Black or Black British		
Caribbean	18,087	7.1%
African	23,037	9.0%
Black other	6,706	2.6%
Arab	2,229	0.9%
Chinese or other		
Chinese	3,744	1.5%
Other ethnic group	9,826	3.9%

Source: London Government Directory: A guide to local government in London (2016). London Communications Agency.

CLLR CHARLES ADJE
Labour Party; White Hart Lane Ward;
1998 - Date

Cllr Charles Adje was elected to Haringey Council in Tottenham's White Hart Lane Ward in 1998. At Haringey, he held the portfolios of *Executive Member for Resources* from 2000 to 2001, *Executive Member for Finance & Support Services* from 2002 to 2003, *Executive Member for Finance 2003-2004* and *Cabinet Member for Resources*. He was elected *Leader of the Council* in May 2004 and subsequently re-elected in May 2005.

Cllr Charles Adje has chaired the *Personnel Sub-Committee* and was a member of the *Haringey Policy & Strategy Committee*. He was the UK's first Council Leader of Nigerian descent.

Currently Chair of the *Housing and Regeneration Scrutiny Panel*, Cllr Charles Adje has a professional background in Human Resources Management and now works as a Human Resources Team Manager with the *London Fire and Emergency Planning Authority*.

Charles is married with one son.

CLLR JOSEPH EJIOFOR
Labour Party; Bruce Grove Ward;
2010 – Date

Cllr Joseph Ejiofor is the Deputy Leader of Haringey Council. He was born in the London Borough of Southwark to Nigerian parents from villages near Owerri in Imo State Nigeria.

Joseph was first elected to Newham Council in 1997, and was re-elected twice more at subsequent elections. After his family moved homes, Joseph stood for election to Haringey Council. He was elected as a Councillor in Bruce Grove Ward in Tottenham in 2010, and re-elected 4 years later.

His colleagues elected him to be the Deputy Leader of Haringey Council in May 2017. He holds the Customer Services portfolio. During his time as a Councillor, he had previously held the Cabinet portfolio for Planning & Enforcement, and was a former Chair of West Green & Bruce Grove Area Assembly. He was also a former Chair of Education Overview & Scrutiny on Newham Council.

Joseph graduated as a mature student with an honours degree in Politics and Government. He is married and the union is blessed with two teenage daughters.

Over the past 18 years, he has worked as a manager in the public, private and the voluntary sectors; specialising in 'risk and performance management' and 'diversity and change management'. Over the past couple of years, Joseph has followed modern business trends and refocused his speciality to iBusiness development.

CLLR MARTHA OSAMOR
Labour Party; Bruce Grove Ward;
1986 - 1990

Cllr Martha Osamor was elected a Labour Councillor and had served form May 1986 to 1990 representing the Bruce Grove Ward in the London Borough of Haringey.

He was a former Deputy Leader Haringey Council and had also served as Chair of *Schools Committee* and Member, *Education Committee*.

Martha Osamor who hails from Delta State, Nigeria, trained as a teacher. She was a community activist, Member of *Unite The Union*, *Co Op Party* and *Labour Party*.

Cllr Osamor was a founder member of *Nigerian Organisation of Women* (NOW), and founder member, *Broadwater Farm Defence Committee*.

She retired as a Legal Adviser at Tottenham Law Centre having previously served as Chair, *Haringey Law Centre.*

Cllr Martha Osamor is also a retired *Trade Union Panel Member, Employment Tribunal*

HARROW BOROUGH

Population 250,800

Ethnicity
White
White British 73,826 30.9%
White Irish 7,336 3.1%
White Gypsy or Irish traveller 181 0.1%
White other 19,648 8.2%

Mixed
White & black Caribbean 2,344 1.0%
White & black African 1,053 0.4%
White & Asian 3,417 1.4%
Mixed others 2,685 1.1%

Asian or Asian British
Indian 63,051 26.4%
Pakistani 7,797 3.3%
Bangladeshi 1,378 0.6%
Asian other 26,953 11.3%

Black or Black British
Caribbean 6,812 2.8%
African 4,370 3.6%
Black other 931 1.8%
Arab 3,708 1.6%

Chinese or other
Chinese 2,629 1.1%
Other ethnic group 3,342 1.4%

CLLR CHIKA AMADI
Edgware Ward; Harrow Council

Cllr (Mrs) Chika Amadi holds a first Bachelor of Arts Degree in History from Abia State University, Abia State. Then a second degree in law (LLB) Law from the Middlesex University and The College of Law London. A Level Three accredited Immigration Law Consultant, together with her husband, they pastor *Goodnews Ministries International Church London*. Chika is also a TV talkshow host - *The Pastor's Wife Talkshow*, a relationship mentor and public speaker.

She has five published books including, *How to Succeed with your Dream*, to her credit. She is a contributing writer to few newspapers including the *Nigerian Guardian Newspaper* as well as Trustee of two charities including *Relate London North West*. In 2010, Chika was awarded a distinguished Service Award as *African Woman of Influence* for her enlightenment work of the younger generation.

Chika was elected Edgware Ward Councillor, London Borough of Harrow. She has served in many capacities including, twice Chief Whip of the Labour Group, member of the *Overview and Scrutiny*, *Licensing Panel* and *Chair of Tarsap* (Traffic and Road Safety

Advisory Panel).

Chika has a passion to speak up for those less able to and to help people discover and fulfil their life ambitions as she believes that everyone deserves to be empowered and given opportunity to achieve great things which can be summarised as : Advocating, inspiring and empowering.

HAVERING BOROUGH

Population	247,000	
Ethnicity		
White		
White British	197,615	83.3%
White Irish	2,989	1.3%
White Gypsy or Irish Traveller	160	0.1%
White other	7,185	3.0%
Mixed		
White & black Caribbean	1,970	0.8%
White & black African	712	0.3%
White & Asian	1,154	0.5%
Mixed others	1,097	0.5%
Asian or Asian British		
Indian	5,017	2.1%
Pakistani	1,492	0.6%
Bangladeshi	975	0.4%
Asian other	2,602	1.1%
Black or Black British		
Caribbean	2,885	1.2%
African	7,581	3.2%
Black other	1,015	0.4%
Arab	311	0.1%
Chinese or other		
Chinese	1,459	0.6%
Other ethnic group	1,013	0.4%

Source: London Government Directory: A guide to local government in London (2016). London Communications Agency.

CLLR WILLIAM ODULATE
Conservative Party; 1978 – 1982
Cllr William Odulate was a Conservative Councillor who represented *Chase Cross Ward* from 1978 to 1982. He was the first Nigerian to be elected in the UK.

LAMBETH BOROUGH

Population	321,300	
Ethnicity		
White		
White British	118,250	39%
White Irish	7,456	2.5%
White Gypsy or Irish Traveller	195	0.1%
White other	47,124	15.5%
Mixed		
White & black Caribbean	8,302	2.7%
White & black African	4,301	1.4%
White & Asian	3,574	1.2%
Mixed others	6,983	2.3%
Asian or Asian British		
Indian	4,983	1.6%
Pakistani	3,072	1.0%
Bangladeshi	2,221	0.7%
Asian other	6,089	2.0%
Black or Black British		
Caribbean	28,886	9.5%
African	35,187	11.6%
Black other	14,469	4.8%
Arab	*1,728*	*0.6%*
Chinese or other		
Chinese	4,573	1.5%
Other ethnic group	5,693	1.9%

Source: London Government Directory: A guide to local government in London (2016). London Communications Agency.

CLLR ADEDAMOLA AMINU

Labour Party; Tulse Hill Ward; 2006 – Date;
Deputy Mayor; 2013/2014
Mayor; 2014/2015

Councillor Adedamola Aminu was elected in 2006 of the Labour Party to represent *Tulse Hill Ward*, Brixton in Lambeth. He is very active politically and was elected as *Deputy Mayor* in 2013 – 2014 and later served as the *Mayor of Lambeth* in 2014 - 2015, thus becoming the first Nigerian to hold that position. Between 2010 and 2013, he was the *Deputy Cabinet Member for Children and Young People*. Cllr Aminu had also served as the *Deputy Cabinet Member for Enterprise* in 2015-2016.

On February 22nd 2017, Cllr Aminu was conferred with honorary Freeman of the City of London.

He is the Chairman of the *Association of Nigerian-British Councillors* in the United Kingdom and President of the *Association of Nigerian Academics UK* (ANAUK). In both of these organisations, he is a founding member.

Cllr Aminu served on the following committees and outside bodies such as *Joint Meeting of the Appointments, Planning, Children and Young People Committee, Equality Impact Assessment Committee, Overview and Scrutiny Committees, School Organisation Advisory Board for the London Borough of Lambeth* and other outside bodies such as *London Councils –*

Children and Young Peoples Forum, Reserve Forces and Cadets Association for Greater London.

He holds a Bachelor's degree with honours in Business Studies from *London Southbank University*, Diploma in Marketing from the *Chartered Institute of Marketing*, a Master's Degree in Marketing from *Greenwich University* and a Post Graduate Certificate in Education (PGCE Cantab).

Cllr Aminu is a lecturer in Business and Computing and is also engaged as a Management Consultant. He has acted as a school governor for various schools and staff governor for Higher Education College as well as being a Trustee for a charitable organisation.

Cllr Adedamola Aminu is a recipient of many awards for leadership and community engagement which includes some of the underlisted.

Cllr Aminu is one of the 100 Outstanding Nigerian-Britons recognized for their excellent contributions to the UK society over the last 100 years at the *Nigerian Centenary Celebrations* in the United Kingdom (2014), Nigerian High Commissioner Award for meritorious services to Nigerian Community in the United Kingdom (2014), *Grassroots Diplomat Honouree* (2015), *Gathering of Africa's Best Award* (2013), *Life Changer Award for Civic Leader* (2013) and *BEFFTA Community Leadership Award* recipient (2015).

CLLR DONATUS ANYANWU

Labour Party; Coldharbour Ward;
1998, 2002 – Date
Deputy Mayor; 2014/2015
Mayor; 2015/2016

Donatus has been a councillor for Angell Town which later became Coldharbour Ward since 1998, and became Mayor of Lambeth in April 2015 having previously been the Deputy Mayor since May 2014. He was Cabinet Member for *Housing, Adult Social Care and Health, Community Safety* and currently Cabinet Member for *Community Relations* and Lead member for Brixton. He was also spokesperson for *Transport and Environment*.

He was member of *Overview and Scrutiny Committee* and Chair of *Adult Social Care and Health Scrutiny Committee* and *Finance Committee*. Donatus has been a senior manager of various third sector organisations, inculding Head of Advice of a national HIV charity.

A graduate of History and Sociology from the University College, Cork (Ireland), he also completed an MA in Diplomatic History.

CLLR FLORENCE ESHALOMI
Labour Party; 2006 - Date

Florence Eshalomi *AM* has been a member of the London Assembly since May 2016. As a representative of the Lambeth and Southwark constituency - covering Streatham, Dulwich and West Norwood, Vauxhall, Peckham and Southwark and Old Bermondsey - Florence strives to put the issues that matter to local people firmly on the political agenda.

A Brixton Hill councillor for 11 years (elected in May 2006) and a former member of Lambeth Council's Cabinet, Florence is well attuned to advocating the needs of local people. During her time as Cabinet member for Culture, Sport and the Olympics, Florence was responsible for the delivery of the hugely popular Lambeth Country Show and chaired the Libraries Commission.

As a former Chair of Lambeth's housing scrutiny committee, Deputy Cabinet member for communities and young people, and special representative for tackling youth violence, Florence has a strong record of tackling the big issues that matter to South Londoners.

Florence resolutely believes public office should be truly representative and has led endeavours to boost youth and black representation in London politics. She led on introducing Lambeth Council's youth mayor elections in 2007 and London Councils' "Be a Councillor" campaign.

Prior to her election, she worked in a range of campaigning, public affairs and policy roles. Florence worked for the *Runnymede Trust*, the UK's leading Race Equality Think Thank. She also worked for *Four Communications* – a leading communications agency, Islington Council and the Labour Party. She is a member of the *London Regional Arts Council UK*.

In her role at City Hall working alongside the Mayor of London and other London Assembly Members, Florence is keen to put the political spotlight firmly on transport, policing, health, housing, equalities, culture, education and businesses.

CLLR LINDA BELLOS
Labour Party; 1986-1990

Linda Bellos was elected as a Labour councillor to the Lambeth London Borough Council in 1985. She was the leader of the council between 1986 and 1988. She was the second black woman to become the leader of a British local authority, after Merle Amory in the north-west London Borough of Brent. Bellos resigned as leader on 21 April 1988 and would be remembered as a prominent figure in left-wing politics in London in the 1980s. She was vice-chair of the successful *Black Sections* campaign to select African-Caribbean and Asian parliamentary and local candidates within the Labour Party.

Bellos was the treasurer of the *Africa Reparations Movement* (UK). She was co-chair of the *Southwark LGBT Network* until February 2007 and an adviser to Southwark Council. From 2000 to 2003, she was co-chair of the *LGBT Advisory Group to the Metropolitan Police*. She remains a community activist.

She has accomplished many firsts in her fight for equality, notably originating the *Black History Month* in the UK while chairing the *London Strategic Policy Unit*.

Bellos has worked on mainstreaming equality within many public bodies, including the British Army and the Metropolitan Police Service. She was an Independent Advisor to the *Metropolitan Police*, the Crown Prosecution Service, and the *Association of Chief Police Officers* (now replaced by *National Police Chiefs' Council* (NPCC). She is a founder member and current Chair of the *Institute of Equality and Diversity Practitioners*.

Bellos provides equality, diversity and human rights consultancy and training services to the UK's commercial, public and not-for-profit sectors. Her company is called Linda Bellos Associates. She now teaches employers and their staff to apply the *Equality Act 2010*, the *Human Rights Act 1998* and other equality laws.

On 9 December 2002, she was presented (together with Stephen Bourne) with the *Metropolitan Police Volunteer Awards* "in recognition of outstanding contribution in supporting the local community."

In 2006, she was awarded an *OBE* in the Queen's New Year's Honours for services to diversity.

CLLR AMANDA INYANG
1982-1986, 1990

CLLR ÀBÁYÒMÍ BURAIMOH-IGBO
1986 – 1990; STREATHAM SOUTH
1990 – 1994; FERNDALE

LEWISHAM BOROUGH

Population   293,900

Ethnicity
White
White British	114,446	41.5%
White Irish	5,206	1.9%
White Gypsy or Irish Traveller	208	0.1%
White other	27,826	10.1%

Mixed
White & black Caribbean	8,539	3.1%
White & black African	3,559	1.3%
White & Asian	3,045	1.1%
Mixed others	5,329	1.9%

Asian or Asian British
Indian	4,600	1.7%
Pakistani	1,596	0.6%
Bangladeshi	1,388	0.5%
Asian other	11,786	4.3%

Black or Black British
Caribbean	30,854	11.2%
African	32,025	11.6%
Black other	12,063	4.4%

Arab   1,456   0.5%

Chinese or other
Chinese	6,164	2.2%
Other ethnic group	5,795	2.1%

Source: London Government Directory: A guide to local government in London (2016). London Communications Agency.

CLLR CRADA ONUEGBU

Labour Party; Evelyn Ward;
2006-28/08/2016

First elected in 2002, Cllr Onuegbu was re-elected in May 2006 representing *Evelyn Ward* in the London Borough of Lewisham. She was a *Cabinet Member for Youth*, *Cabinet Member for Community Safety* and chair of *London Fire and Emergency Planning Authority*'s strategy committee.

Cllr Crada served on the following committees: *Constitution Working Committee*, *Lewisham Community/Police Consultative Group*, *Corporate Parenting Group*, *Local Authorities Action for South Africa- National Steering Committee*, *Community Safety & Policing Forum*.

Cllr Onuegbu passed away on Sunday 28th August 2016 and has been described as a long-serving councillor who did her best to improve the lot of her constituents.

CLLR OBAJIMI ADEFIRANYE

Labour Party; Brockley Ward; 2014 – Date

Councillor Obajimi Adefiranye is currently Chair of the Council. He represents *Brockley Ward*. His other committee appointments include: *Brockley Assembly*, *Constitution Working Party*, *Council Urgency*, *Overview and Scrutiny Committee*, *Planning Committee A* and the *Standards Committee*.

CLLR RACHEL ONIKOSI

Labour Party; Sydenham Ward; 2014 – Date
Elected in 2014 to represent *Sydenham Ward*, Cllr Onikosi has served on the following committees: *Mayor and Cabinet, Mayor and Cabinet (Contracts), Sydenham Assembly Appointments to outside bodies, London Council's Transport & Environment Committee, South East London Waste Disposal Group* and *Works Council*. She currently holds the position of *Cabinet Member Public Realm*.

CLLR OLUROTIMI OGUNBADEWA

Labour Party; Downham Ward; 2014 - Date
Councillor Olurotimi Ogunbadewa was elected in 2014 to represent *Downham Ward*. He has since his election served on the following committees: *Downham Assembly, Housing Select Committee, Overview and Scrutiny Committee, Pensions Investment Committee* and the *Planning Committee B* of which he was Vice-Chair.

CLLR SAMUEL OWOLABI-OLUYOLE

Labour Party; Evelyn Ward; 01/05/2006 - 06/01/2014

Elected in 2006 to represent *Evelyn Ward*, Cllr Owolabi-Oluyole served on the following Committees: *Election Committee, Standard Committee, Constitution Working Committee, Sustainable Development, Housing, Albany 2001 Council of Management, Housing Joint Partnership* and *Planning Committee*.

CLLR ANNE AFFIKU

Labour Party; Forest Hill; 2010 - 2014

She was elected in 2010 to represent *Forest Hill*. Cllr Affiku served on several committees, including *Healthier Communities, Forest Hill & Sydenham Voluntary Service Association* and the *Lewisham Disability Coalition*.

CLLR JOSEPH FOLORUNSO
Labour Party; Evelyn Ward;
2010 – 20/02/2013
Councillor Joseph Folorunso was elected in 2010 and represented *Evelyn Ward*. During his tenure, he had served on the following committees: *Healthier Communities, Safer & Stronger Communities, Lewisham Citizen's Advice Bureau Management Committee* and the *Planning Committee*.

CLLR OLUFUNKE ABIDOYE
Labour Party; Evelyn Ward;
28/03/2013 - 26/05/2014
Elected to represent *Evelyn Ward* in a bye-election. She is a trained and qualified nurse.

LABOUR PARTY; HORNIMAN WARD; 1994 TAYO OKE

MERTON BOROUGH

Population	210,300	
Ethnicity		
White		
White British	96,658	48.4%
White Irish	4,417	2.2%
White Gypsy or Irish Traveller	216	0.1%
White other	28,315	14.2%
Mixed		
White & black Caribbean	2,579	1.3%
White & black African	1,279	1.5%
White & Asian	2,829	0.6%
Mixed others	2,647	1.3%
Asian or Asian British		
Indian	8,106	4.1%
Pakistani	7,337	3.7%
Bangladeshi	2,216	1.1%
Asian other	15,866	7.9%
Black or Black British		
Caribbean	8,126	4.1%
African	10,442	5.2%
Black other	2,243	1.1%
Arab	1,413	0.7%
Chinese or other		
Chinese	2,618	1.3%
Other ethnic group	3,386	1.2%

Source: London Government Directory: A guide to local government in London (2016). London Communications Agency.

CLLR GREGORY PATRICK UDEH

Labour Party; Graveney Ward; 2006 - Date

Elected in 2006 and representing *Graveney Ward*. Cllr Udeh's Committee appointments are: *Council, Healthier Communities and Older People Overview and Scrutiny Panel* (Substitute), *Licensing Committee, South West London Joint Health Overview and Scrutiny Committee* (Substitute) and *Standards and General Purposes Committee*.

CLLR FIDELIS GADZAMA

Labour Party; Cannon Hill Ward; 2014 to Date

Athlete and Olympic medallist, Fidelis Gadzama was elected as a Labour councillor in May 2014 for the *Cannon Hill Ward*. Cllr Gadzama was in the relay team (4x400 metres) that won a silver medal at the 2000 Olympics in Sydney. After the victory of the USA team which won gold was overturned as a result of doping and the team stripped of its gold, Gadzama and his team were re-allocated the gold medal.

His committee appointments are Council and Joint Consultative Committee with Ethnic Minority Organisations.

Source: Wikipedia

MILTON KEYNES BOROUGH

CLLR TUBO URANTA
Conservative Party; Elected 2014 to date

Cllr Uranta is a Business Consultant who has worked across industries as well as with the NHS and Primary Care Group (GPs, CCGs) for over 20 years. He got into politics in the UK in 2008 and has passionately followed this line of career pursuit since then. His dream is of a better Nigeria, although he also wants to be part of his community here in the United Kingdom, help his Nigerian families here in UK and develop a personal pursuit of knowledge power (intellectual property).

In pursuit of his career interests, he was first nominated to become a Parish Councillor in 2014 and was subsequently elected in the 2015 elections. His overall goal is to keep building a knowledge block for himself and help his community here in UK to succeed in both individual goals as well as communal pursuits.

NEWHAM BOROUGH

Population	330,300	
Ethnicity		
White		
White British	51,516	16.7%
White Irish	2,172	0.7%
White Gypsy or Irish Traveller	462	0.2%
White other	35,066	11.4%
Mixed		
White & black Caribbean	3,957	1.3%
White & black African	3,319	1.1%
White & Asian	2,677	0.9%
Mixed others	3,992	1.3%
Asian or Asian British		
Indian	42,484	13.8%
Pakistani	30,307	9.8%
Bangladeshi	37,262	12.1%
Asian other	19,912	6.5%
Black or Black British		
Caribbean	15,050	4.9%
African	37,811	12.3%
Black other	7,395	2.4%
Arab	3,523	1.1%
Chinese or other		
Chinese	3,930	1.3%
Other ethnic group	7,149	2.3%

Source: London Government Directory: A guide to local government in London (2016), London Communications Agency.

CLLR JOY LAGUDA *MBE*
Labour; Plaistow North Ward

Councillor Joy Laguda MBE was elected on the platform of the Labour Party. Widely experienced, she has served as *Associate Cabinet Member and Mayoral Advisor - Adults Safeguarding* and *Chair of Council.* Cllr Laguda's committee appointments include: *Chief Officer Appointment Committee, Chief Officer Appointments Sub-Committee, Joint Meeting of Committees, Standards Advisory Committee* and the *Standards Advisory Committee (Hearing) Sub-Committee.*

A nurse by profession, Cllr Laguda has lived in Plaistow for 25 years. She has been a governor for most improved local primary school for 16 years, and works closely with local residents, consulting on the priority issues. Joy is a member of the *Rotary Club of Newham*, and has been awarded an MBE by Her Majesty the Queen for services rendered in community work.

CLLR CHARITY FIBERESIMA
Labour Party; Plaistow South Ward & later Boleyn Ward; 2010 - 2015

Charity Fiberesima was first elected as a Labour councillor in *Plaistow South Ward* in 2010, and then the *Boleyn Ward* in 2014.

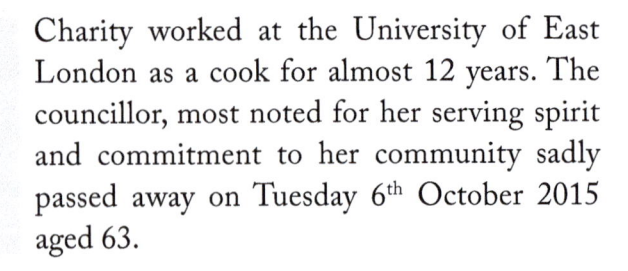

Charity worked at the University of East London as a cook for almost 12 years. The councillor, most noted for her serving spirit and commitment to her community sadly passed away on Tuesday 6th October 2015 aged 63.

CLLR SEYI AKINWOWO
Labour Party; Forest Gate North Ward; 2014 - Date

Cllr Seyi Akiwowo, Newham Council's youngest representative, was elected 2014 on the platform of Labour. Having lived in Newham for over 20 years, Cllr Akiwowo has volunteered in various capacities including serving on the *Newham Youth Council* in 2008 and *UK Youth Parliament* in 2009. She is a BSc Social Policy graduate of the *London School of Economics* (LSE) and school governor at Kay Rowe Nursery in a Forest Gate. Seyi has been a member of the Labour Party since the age of 16 because she strongly believes in its social justice values.

She is currently Deputy Chair of the *Crime & Anti-Social Behaviour Scrutiny Commission* and Member of the *Duke of Edinburgh's Award Committee* in Newham. She is affiliated to the following committees: *Investment & Accounts*

Committee, Overview & Scrutiny Committee, Budget Working Party and *Crime & Anti-Social Behaviour Scrutiny Commission.*
Other projects involved in included the *Domestic & Sexual Violence Members Steering Group* and *Forest Gate Community Neighbourhood Forum.* Cllr Seyi Akiwowo is very active in community engagements and charity works, hence her being involved with the *Forest Gate Women's Institute, Newham Black History Month Standing Committee* and as Chair of *West Ham Constituency Labour Party Women's Forum.*
Outside her council duties, Cllr Akiwowo works for a UK Education Charity. She also blogs on education policy reforms and is an active member of Hillsong Church London.,

CLLR SIMEON ADEWOLE ADEMOLAKE
Christian People's Alliance Party;
Canning Town South Ward; 1996 – 2010
Simeon studied Urban and Regional Planning in Yaba College of Technology where he was elected the President and the Chairman of the Standing Committee of the Students Union. He later studied Law at University of East London and CPD in Learning Skills in

Middlesex University. A former president of the Students Union in Yaba College of Technology, Simeon stood as a parliamentary candidate for the Christian Peoples' Alliance in the 2005 General Election unfortunately he lost to Jim Fitzpatrick MP.

But in 2006, Simeon was selected to run as a local councillor. He won a councillor seat in Newham, so ending 100 years of Labour dominance in Canning Town South. His victory was historic; with Simeon becoming the first ever black to be elected as an opposition councillor in Newham, and on the National stage, He is the first and only black so far to be elected by a Christian Democratic Party in British electoral history. Since becoming a councillor, Simeon has successfully changed Newham Council's policy of involvement with supplementary education, after his motion was unanimously supported by all councillors and Newham executive Mayor.

In March 2007, Simeon made National Head line, Captioned "Victory for Motorist" by the Evening Standard. He won a land mark case over London Transport's attempt to illegally penalise motorist by issuing illegal parking ticket. The outcome of this case brought transparency into the parking law and the need for photographic evidence to be produced before a parking ticket is deemed valid nationally. Simeon in effect, is the reason why all parking attendant all over the Country must carry a digital camera today. Simeon appeared on BBC Breakfast News enlighten motorist on their rights.

Simeon had started life in the UK as a menswear label owner, and this garnered him an astounding success with an impressive list of clients with the business also expanding into a Training School.

In 2014 Simeon was unanimously elected as the Chairman of Newham Partnership for Supplementary School. His mission as the leader of this partnership is to unite all Supplementary Schools. Simeon pioneered the first Supplementary School week in Newham Borough bringing together many nationalities and Supplementary schools.

Cllr Ademolake is a family man to the core, a teacher, a mentor and a business coach.

Simeon joined The Redeemed Christian Church of God in 1998, and in 2007, he was sent to pastor a branch (Harvest Chapel situated in Plaistow London), where he is the resident pastor.

His passion includes meeting people, politics, preaching and empowerment.

SOUTHWARK BOROUGH

Population	306,500	
Ethnicity		
White		
White British	114,534	39.7%
White Irish	6,222	2.2%
White Gypsy or Irish Traveller	263	0.1%
White other	35,330	12.3%
Mixed		
White & black Caribbean	5,677	2.0%
White & black African	3,687	1.3%
White & Asian	3,003	1.0%
Mixed others	5,411	1.9%
Asian or Asian British		
Indian	5,819	2.0%
Pakistani	1,623	0.6%
Bangladeshi	3,912	1.4%
Asian other	7,764	2.7%
Black or Black British		
Caribbean	17,974	6.2%
African	47,413	16.4%
Black other	12,124	4.2%
Arab	2,440	0.8%
Chinese or other		
Chinese	8,074	2.8%
Other ethnic group	7,013	2.4%

Source: London Government Directory: A guide to local government in London (2016). London Communications Agency.

CLLR TAYO SITU

Labour Party; 2002 – 9th May 2011

Cllr Tayo Situ was elected Mayor of Southwark at the *Annual Meeting of Council Assembly* on 19 May 2010. Educated at *The Polytechnic Ibadan*, Nigeria and with a background in Economics before settling in the UK in 1985, Cllr Situ later attended the *Guildhall* and *South Bank* Universities studying accountancy. He was a trustee and volunteer on many organisations and represented the local community for many years before being elected to the Council in 2002, representing Peckham ward.

Devoted to job creation for the community members and making services and infrastructures affordable and available to the locals, he was the founding member of *Association of British-Nigerian Councillors* and the first Chairman. Cllr Tayo Situ passed away on 9th May 2011.

CLLR MICHAEL SITU

Labour Party; Livesey Ward; 2010 - Date

Michael Situ is a councillor in Southwark. He was elected in 2010. He has held the role of Cabinet Member with responsibility for *Communities and Safety* and oversaw Southwark Council's work on combating extremism and child sexual exploitation. Cllr Michael Situ also worked on the introduction of a new Women's Safety Charter, Domestic Abuse Strategy, and tightening up the Borough's licensing policy to make it pleasant for everyone going out at night. Having worked within the criminal justice system over the last six years as a lawyer, he is all too aware of the importance of creating an environment where people can feel safe to live, study or work. He has held roles within community life including being a School Governor, Chair of the *Tayo Situ Foundation* and Trustee of many local organisations.

CLLR THE RIGHT REVEREND EMMANUEL OYEWOLE

Labour; Camberwell Green Ward; 2010 - 2014

Cllr The Right Reverend Oyewole is a trade unionist and has a sound knowledge of, and has worked for several years in the Health and Social Services field especially, in the area of

Support and Health & Safety compliance.

Cllr The Right Reverend Oyewole was the chair of *Peckham Area Forum*. He was an executive member of the *Southwark Group of Tenants Organisation* and the Chair of *Acorn Tenants and Residents Association*.

He had held several positions before he was elected as the Councillor for Camberwell Green Ward in Camberwell and Peckham Constituency in May 2010. In May 2012, he was appointed as the Deputy Cabinet Member for *Southwark Faith Communities* while in the previous municipal year, he was appointed as the Deputy Cabinet Member for *Southwark Heritage* for the municipal Year 2011/12. He served as the Deputy Cabinet Member for *Faith Communities* for the municipal years 2012 - 2014. Also, he was appointed as the Chair of *Planning Sub-Committee A* and Vice Chair of *Education, Children's Services and Leisure Scrutiny Sub-Committee*. He was also a member of the *Overview Scrutiny Committee, Licensing Committee, Health and Adult Social Care, Communities and Citizenship Scrutiny Sub-Committee, Standing Advisory Council on Religious Education, Leaseholder Arbitration and Tenancy Agreement Arbitration Panel*.

He is currently the chair of *WiseGem*, a

charity organisation based in Peckham which supports families to tackle teenage pregnancies and cope with life after childbirth in Southwark and also a member and working group panel of *Southwark Neighbourhood Board*. He was appointed as the Chairman for *London 2013* for London Borough of Southwark also an Executive member of *Southwark Police and Community Consultative Group* (UK) in 2012.

Cllr The Right Rev Oyewole has also been involved in several other community engagements, including: *Southwark Black History Month*, *Southwark Police and Community Consultative Group* (UK), *Southwark Neighbourhood Board* and *Kiwanis Central London*.

CLLR MICHAEL BUKOLA
Liberal Democrats Party;
South Bermondsey Ward; 2010 - 2014

Cllr Michael Bukola was elected in 2010 to represent South Bermondsey Ward in Southwark under the platform of the Liberal Democrats Party. His professional background is as a tax adviser with *Deloitte & Touche* in London. He advised *FTSE 100* & *Dow 50* multinational corporations on strategic and operational tax planning to help clients streamline and improve their bottom line. Michael was a school governor and trustee of local charities *Blackfriars Settlement* and *Volunteer Centre Southwark*.

He stood as a Parliamentary Candidate for Lewisham Deptford in the last General Election 2015.

CLLR SUNNY LAMBE

Labour Party; South Bermondsey Ward; 2014 – Date

Cllr. Sunny Lambe, *DipM, FCIM, MBA, PGCEFE*, Chartered Marketer, holds the position of Backbencher and sits on the *Licensing and Education Committee* in Southwark Council. Some of his works in public service reflect on his background. He is a community leader, publisher of *Ethno News* magazine and a business management consultant with over 20 years' experience ranging from general business enterprise management, advice, lectureships, and consultancy services covering public, private and community/voluntary (social enterprises) sectors.

He is actively involved in the youth, employment, business and enterprise projects.

His brainchild, the *Basic Business Initiative UK* (BBI the UK) which he started in 2001 and where he also serves as the Executive Director, is a charitable enterprise support agency committed to promoting entrepreneurship and self-economic empowerment, with a strong passion for entrepreneurs, youth development, promotion of diversity and achievement. He is also the founder and executive director of a consulting firm, *SAL Associates Ltd.* Cllr. Lambe's other projects include the *African People's Forum, Black Business Awards, Young Entrepreneur Game Award* and the *Ethnic Business Network.*

Sunny also volunteers his time and skills to a significant number of community initiatives such as school governorships. He was formerly Lay Chair of *Church of England Camberwell Deanery Synod,* Vice Chair of *Southwark Alliance Enterprise Partnership Board,* Member of *Labour Party International Development Advisory Task Group* (chaired by Rt. Hon. Harriet Harman QC MP), member of *Southwark Liberal Democratic Party Equality Policy Review Task Group, Southwark Local Economy Group, Local Enterprise Task Group,* and member of governing bodies/strategy working groups of some schools and colleges. On 13 May 2006, Sunny became a recipient of Southwark Civic Award '*Honorary Liberty of the Old Metropolitan Borough of Camberwell*' including *Honorary Liberty of the Old Metropolitan Borough of Southwark for BBI UK* in May 2012, awarded by *Southwark Council Civic Association* for his civic contributions to the borough.

CLLR JOHNSON SITU
Labour Party; Peckham ward; 2014 - Date

Cllr Johnson Situ is Cabinet member for *Business, Culture and Social Regeneration* with responsibility for promoting business growth and employment across Southwark. Alongside that, he has the responsibility for developing arts and culture in the borough, including museums, heritage and libraries.

Cllr Johnson Situ was elected as a Councillor for Peckham Ward in May 2014. Before joining the cabinet, he worked in the international development sector, for *Comic Relief*, *Disaster Emergency Committee* and *Room to Read*. He is a member of the *Chartered Institute of Public Relations*, and when not working, he is an avid football fan.

CLLR JAMES OKOSUN
Liberal Democrats Party; Surrey Docks Ward; 2014 - Date

Cllr James is a Liberal Democrats councillor. Elected in 2014 to represent Surrey Docks, he is a qualified social worker. An astute community campaigner, one of his major areas of focus is acting as spokesman on children and young people.

CLLR ADEDOKUN LASAKI
Liberal Democrats Party; South Bermondsey Ward; 2006 - 2010

Adedokun Lasaki, an Owu prince from the Otileta ruling house in Abeokuta was elected councillor on the platform of Liberal Democrats to represent South Bermondsey Ward in the London Borough of Southwark in April 2006. He served for 4 years ending in 2010

He was Chair of Health and Adult Care Scrutiny Committee for two years (2008 and 2009).

His venture into politics was not his first involvement in the community he lived in.

He was a member of Tenant Council for 10 years, Chair of Decima Street Tenants and

Residents Association and the Treasurer and Director of Leathermarket Joint Management Board – one of the biggest Tenants Managed Organisations (TMO) in the UK – for 10 years.

CLLR OLAJUMOKE RISIKAT OYEWUNMI
Labour Party; Peckham Ward; 2006 - 2010

CLLR JELIL LADIPO
Liberal Democrats Party; Newington Ward; 2006 - 2010

LABOUR PARTY; LIDDLE WARD; 1994 ABDUR-RAHMAN O. OLAYIWOLA

WALTHAM FOREST BOROUGH

Population	272,000	
Ethnicity		
White		
White British	92,999	36.0%
White Irish	3,959	1.5%
White Gypsy or Irish Traveller	369	0.1%
White other	37,472	14.5%
Mixed		
White & black Caribbean	4,568	1.8%
White & black African	2,403	0.9%
White & Asian	2,602	1.0%
Mixed others	4,193	1.6%
Asian or Asian British		
Indian	9,134	3.5%
Pakistani	26,347	10.2%
Bangladeshi	4,632	1.8%
Asian other	11,697	4.5%
Black or Black British		
Caribbean	18,841	7.3%
African	18,815	7.3%
Black other	7,135	2.8%
Arab	3,776	1.5%
Chinese or other		
Chinese	2,579	1.0%
Other ethnic group	6,728	2.6%

Source: London Government Directory: A guide to local government in London (2016). London Communications Agency.

CLLR ANNA MBACHU
Labour Party; Grove Green Ward;
2006 - Date
Mayor; 2009/2010

Anna Mbachu originates from Mbachu Family (Umuduruebo) Okwelle in Imo State. She is married to Dozie Ogbuebile of Irete in Owerri West LGA of Imo State. Councillor Anna Mbachu was first elected into office in May 2006 representing Grove Green Ward in London Borough of Waltham Forest in United Kingdom.

She represents a new style of Black leaders that are diplomatic, methodical with a can do attitude, which has set her apart from the rest. These qualities have earned her a place in history as the first black elected female branch chair of the Labour Party, the first black female Mayor of London Borough of Waltham Forest, first female Mayor of Igbo descent in London, and also the first black elected member of the Cabinet and leadership team. In addition, Councillor Mbachu is a Senior Practicing Clinician/Manager with the National Health Service (NHS) Trust, the Deputy Leader of Waltham Forest Group, Chair of the Boroughs' Housing Scrutiny.

Councillor Mbachu has been listed among other female world leaders and legislators as a role model. In recognition of these, the Nigeria High Commission during the 54th Independence Day celebration which took place on the 4th of October 2014, for the first time in its history, recognised 26 Nigerians from all works of life with an award, to which Cllr. Mbachu was one of the recipients.

She supports a number of charities both locally and internationally. The Councillor is also a recipient of numerous awards and accolades from around the globe. She is married with children one of whom as a teenager became the youngest Councillor in United Kingdom, whilst still pursuing a medical degree.

ELIZABETH ATINUKE ADEBUTU AKA COUNCILLOR DAVIES
Labour Party; Lea Bridge Ward; 2006 - 2014
Atinuke is a qualified social worker. Holding a Master's degree in Social Policy and a postgraduate Diploma in Social Work, she has worked extensively in most London Boroughs' Social Services Departments

Atinuke is a former councillor from London Borough of Waltham Forest, having served as one of the law makers for two terms between 2006 to 2014. Atinuke was very active, within the role creating a number of projects within and outside the borough, that mainly focused on Child Safety (Safeguarding) and assisting vulnerable people in the borough to access services that would enable them to lead independent lives.

With her professional background in social policy and social work, she was able to guide the borough's social services department to increase standards of care which helped to raise ratings.

Atinuke founded, two policy groups which directly advised the former prime ministers Tony Blair and David Cameron on employment concerning Africans in the UK, in order to secure business grants for that ethnic group.

Atinuke has consulted for a number of international and national charity organisations, such as *Amnesty International, Water Aid, NSPCC* etc. on strategy concerning the safeguarding of children. Atinuke has spoken at the *Royal Institute for International Affairs*, the *Commonwealth Institute* and the *Council of Foreign Relations* concerning child trafficking, migration and safeguarding of African children.

Atinuke is currently working as a social policy consultant here in the UK and also in Nigeria.

CLLR WHITNEY IHENACHOR
Labour Party; Leyton Ward; 2014 - Date

Councillor Whitney Ihenachor was first elected in May 2014, representing where she was born and raised, Leyton Ward in the London Borough of Waltham Forest.

Currently the youngest councillor in Waltham Forest, she stands for the dynamic voice of the youth, not only in Leyton but Waltham Forest. Cllr. Whitney represents a driven, confident black female role model that not only the young look up to but those of older generations can also relate.

Moreover, Whitney is currently studying Anatomy at the School of Medicine. She holds the position of Junior Whip on the Council in addition to serving on the *Budget Scrutiny Committee.*

CLLR YEMI OSHO
Labour Party; Lea Bridge Ward; 2014 - Date

Cllr Yemisi Osho was elected as a councillor for Lea Bridge Ward, London Borough of Waltham Forest in 2014. She was elected as The Worshipful Mayor of Waltham Forest May 2017. From early childhood she has always been interested in caring for people as her innate desire is to make a difference in people's life. Hence, after her secondary school education she made a decision to become a nurse although she initially rained as a Midwife. Her nursing career span over 30 years and has worked in various capacities including senior management and board roles in the NHS. She has served on two CCG boards in London and Director of Nursing and Operation.

She has also worked as Regional Officer with the Royal College of Nursing (RCN) and co-pioneer of RCN BME Nurses Forum. She support nurses with work-related stress and disability. She is the founder Ivory Health Foundation and Executive Director of consulting organisation leading on health care policy, sustainable development and transformational change both nationally and internationally.

Cllr Yemisi Osho was awarded Queen's Nurse Title in 2012 by the Queen's Nursing Institute in recognition of her leadership and commitment to providing high quality care to patients. She was also the first to receive National 'Activist of the Year' award in 2013 by Movement for Change in recognition of her philanthropic and charitable work in supporting less privilege in the community to achieve health and well being. Other relevant achievements includes: Elected member of Royal College of Nursing London Regional Board, Chair Waltham Forest Women in Public Life, Vice Chair of Coop Party, Vice Chair CLP, Vice Chair & Secretary of Local Campaign Forum and Member of Chief Nursing Officer BME Advisory Group, NHS England.

Having been elected as Mayor in May 2017 gives her further opportunity and platform to bring diverse cultures together. She has challenged injustice and promoted equality and believed that she has broken glass ceiling against the backdrops of impossibility and barriers.

For over 30 years, she has been an activist and involved in challenging injustice, racial discrimination and active protector of women's rights and empowering others. The overt and covert prejudices that she has experienced; whether on the grounds of race or gender have always strengthened her. As with all things that have arisen in her life, along with the challenges have come excellent opportunities and some absolutely brilliantly supportive people.

During her term as Mayor of Waltham Forest, her theme for the year is Service, Courage and Hope. Her charity is Diabetes

UK and she planned to raise funds to support Local Diabetic service and raise awareness through recruitment of Diabetic champions. Diabetes is the fastest-growing health threat facing UK. The fact that diabetes is a condition that cut across all ages and diverse culture and ethnicity is the reason she choose to fundraise as of her mayoral charity. She believes that if one person is saved from developing kidney failure due to diabetic complications and stress of undergoing potential dialysis which may cost treatment up to £30,000 per annum, we would have made a significant difference in a person's life.

CLLR BABTUNDE DAVIES-ADEBUTU

Labour Party; Cann Hall Ward; 2010 - 2014
Babatunde was born and raised in England, and started his early education at Gatehouse School. For his secondary and A-Level education, he attended the Trinity Catholic High School before proceeding to Bristol University, studying for a combined Law and International Relations degree. He later attended the Inns of Court School of Law.

Tunde Davies-Adebutu was elected as a councillor in the year 2010-2014 at the

London Borough Waltham Forest.

Tunde is a trained Barrister, but currently works as a legal consultant for several private sector companies in the United Kingdom.

During Tunde's time as a councillor in Waltham Forest, he served as the chair of Environment Scrutiny and also the deputy chair of communities and housing, creating a number of projects for the constituents, to access employment and vocational education
.

WANDSWORTH BOROUGH

Population	317,000	
Ethnicity		
White		
White British	163,739	53.3%
White Irish	7,664	2.5%
White Gypsy or Irish Traveller	163	0.1%
White other	47,650	15.5%
Mixed		
White & black Caribbean	4,642	1.5%
White & black African	2,034	0.7%
White & Asian	3,887	1.3%
Mixed others	4,678	1.5%
Asian or Asian British		
Indian	8,642	2.8%
Pakistani	9,718	3.2%
Bangladeshi	1,493	0.5%
Asian other	9,770	3.2%
Black or Black British		
Caribbean	12,297	4.0%
African	14,818	4.8%
Black other	5,641	1.8%
Arab	2,350	0.8%
Chinese or other		
Chinese	3,715	1.2%
Other ethnic group	4,094	1.3%

Source: London Government Directory: A guide to local government in London (2016). London Communications Agency.

HON. ALDERMAN ERELU LOLA AYONRINDE

Conservative Party; Councillor, 1996-2005 Deputy Mayor 1996-1997, Mayor; 1999-2000, 2004-2005

Erelu (Mrs.) Lola Ayonrinde, became the first African Mayor of the south London Borough of Wandsworth in May 1999, elected on the platform of the Conservative Party. Wandsworth, with a population of 317,000, is one of the most affluent boroughs in Britain and mostly populated by white Britons. Ayonrinde was Deputy Mayor between 1996 and 1997 and had served the borough in various local committees. Erelu Ayonrinde was bestowed with the lifetime title of Honorary Alderman in recognition of her distinguished contributions to civic life.

Westminster Borough

Population 232,600

Ethnicity
White
White British	77,334	35.2%
White Irish	4,960	2.3%
White Gypsy or Irish Traveller	76	0.0%
White other	52,960	24.1%

Mixed
White & Black Caribbean	1,869	0.9%
White & Black African	1,927	0.9%
White & Asian	3,584	1.6%
Mixed other	4,015	1.8%

Asian or Asian British
Indian	7,213	3.3%
Pakistani	2,328	1.1%
Bangladeshi	8,299	2.9%
Asian other	10,105	4.6%

Black or Black British
Caribbean	4,449	2.0%
African	9,141	4.2%
Black other	2,882	1.3%

Arab 15,724 7.2%

Chinese or other
Chinese	5,917	2.7%
Other ethnic group	8,613	3.9%

Source: London Government Directory: A guide to local government in London (2016). London Communications Agency.

CLLR DAVID OBAZE

Labour Party; Little Venice ward; 1986 – 1990

David Obaze came to London from Nigeria to qualify and work as an osteopath and naturopath. A former Labour Councillor for Westminster Council, David is now involved with various charities. He is Director of the *National Coalition for Black Volunteering* and a Committee Member of the *Westminster Society*, as well as working with the *Black and Ethnic Minority Diabetes Association (BEMDA)*, *Victim Support London* and *Westminster Citizens Advice*. Cllr Obaze is a Trustee of *The Citizens Trust*, an organisation which promotes inclusion and offer support to all cadres of disadvantaged people in the United Kingdom.

Source: http://www.thecitizenstrust.org.uk/what-we-do/

DISTRICT COUNCILS

BRACKNELL FOREST BOROUGH COUNCIL

Population 113,205

Ethnicity
White
White British	96,080	84.9%
White Irish	984	0.9%
White Gypsy or Irish Traveller	118	0.1%
White other	5,372	4.7%

Mixed
White & black Caribbean	656	0.6%
White & black African	297	0.3%
White & Asian	808	0.7%
Mixed others	542	0.5%

Asian or Asian British
Indian	1,989	1.8%
Pakistani	518	0.5%
Bangladeshi	134	0.3%
Asian other	2,467	0.7%

Black or Black British
Caribbean	404	0.4%
African	1,586	1.4%
Black other	201	0.2%

Arab 201 0.2%

Chinese or other
Chinese	556	0.5%
Other ethnic group	294	0.3%

Source: London Government Directory: A guide to local government in London (2016). London Communications Agency.

CLLR MICHAEL ADENIYI GBADEBO

Conservative Party; Great Hollands North Town Ward; 2011 to 2015

Cllr Michael Gbadebo's passion for services to the community led him to become a councillor in Bracknell Forest, Berkshire (elected to both the borough and town councils) and a governor of the local college *Bracknell & Wokingham College*.

Cllr Michael Adeniyi Gbadebo was elected on the platform of Conservative Party in 2011 and has served on the following committees: *Children, Young People & Learning Overview & Scrutiny Panel, Environment, Culture and Communities Overview & Scrutiny Panel, Licensing and Safety Committee, Planning & Highways Committee, Planning Committee, Overview and Scrutiny Commission, Jennett's Park Community Association, Great Hollands Neighbourhood Action Group, HomeStart Bracknell Forest and Bracknell Enterprise & Innovation Hub*.

Cllr Gbadebo also served in the following capacities within the times stated: *School Governor at Sandhurst Secondary School* (2008 - 2013); Trustee of *Homestart Bracknell Forest* (2010 – 2015); College Governor at *Bracknell and Wokingham College* (2011- 2015) and serving as Chairman of *Bracknell Conservative Association* (2015)

An entrepreneur, technology evangelist and a natural leader with more than 25 years' experience in the information technology industry, he is the CEO of *Creotec Limited*, Michael is a highly motivated and resourceful Internet and business technology strategist, a web application developer with expertise in design, development and implementation of technology solutions in enhancing organisational goals and objectives.

Over the years, has worked with many companies and organisations in Europe, USA, and Africa. These include *Dell UK, exentric Plc, 4Soft UK, Harper Collins, Pratham UK, Anglian Water Services, The Spirit Group, Proxim Wireless USA, Grupo Pinar Spain, Mobell UK, Ernst & Young,* and *Hornby* (*scaletrix*). Others include: *Samsung, Max Lock Centre* (University of Westminster), *SG Hambros Banking, Skibo Castle, Blauverd Habitat, Currencies Direct, Association of Licensed Aircraft Engineers, Chello Broadband, Cass Business School, AWG Plc, HiFX, Nottingham City Council, GlucoMen*, and much more.

CHESHIRE EAST COUNCIL

CLLR IRENE FASEYI
Labour Party; Crewe Central Ward;
2011 – Date
Mayor of Crewe Town Council, 2013/14

Cllr Irene Faseyi represents Crewe Central Ward in Cheshire East Borough Council. Elected on the platform of the Labour Party, Irene was first elected in 2011 and then re-elected in 2015.

She has served in various capacities since her debut election. Her committee appointments have included: Appeals Sub-Committee, Children & Families Overview & Scrutiny Committee, Council and Licensing Committee.

She also serves on the Standing Advisory Council on Religious Education (SACRE), a statutory organisation.

A Registered General Nursing (RGN) practitioner, Cllr Faseyi served as the Mayor of the Crewe Town Council for the 2013/2014 municipal year.

HERTSMERE BOROUGH COUNCIL
(BOREHAMWOOD- KENILWORTH)

CLLR VICTOR O ENI
Conservative Party elected 2015 to date
Cllr Eni is Deputy Mayor of Elstree and Borehamwood for the municipal year 2017/18 for the Hertsmere Borough Council. He holds the traditional title of *Ikemba Aro of Arochukwu*.

He serves in the Personnel and Operation Scrutiny Committees. Aside being a School Governor, Cllr Victor Eni also serves on the following organisations: Chairman, *Amannagwu Community Association UK*, Former Assistance Secretary Nzuko Aro UK, Committee member *Hertsmere Neighbourhood Watch*, Executive member *Hertsmere Conservative Association* and Member Borehamwood and Elstree Twin Town Association.

LEWES DISTRICT COUNCIL

CLLR SAM ADENIJI
Conservative Party;
Seaford South; May 2011- Date
Cllr Sam Adeniji was elected in May 2011 representing Seaford South. He was a *Conservative* from 10 May 2011 to 2 April 2014, *Independent* 2 April to 2 July 2014 and now *Conservative* from 2 July to date. He served as Deputy Leader of the Independent Group from 3rd April 2014 to 2nd July 2014

Source: www.lewesconservatives.com/people/sam-adeniji

MANCHESTER CITY COUNCIL

COUNCILLOR TUTU EKO (PRINCE)
City of Manchester Borough
Labour Party; 1992 - 1996

Been the first Nigerian (Lagosian) to be elected in the City of Manchester has given Cllr Tutu Eko (Prince) a lot of opportunities of working and meeting the needs of pressure groups and in promoting different cultures to the host community.

In 1992, he was appointed to the post of Deputy Chair for Equal Opportunities & Anti-discrimination Committee. This committee is one of the major committees that cater for ethnic groups, anti racist/sexist groups, disable groups and generally promoting anti-discrimination work in the city, making the city a zero tolerance. He was also affiliated to the following committees: *Social Services Committee; Education Committee* and the *Highway Committee.*

Other committees served in council included: *Education; Social Services; Planning and Environment and Licensing Leisure Services Committee.* Cllr Eko also sat as an appeal member in *South Manchester Valuation Appeal Committee*.

During his time in council, he had worked very closely with ethnic groups promoting equal opportunities and had also served as a Chairperson for *North Manchester Law Centre* dealing with immigration problems, housing, social benefits and day to day problems.

His community engagements, cultural activism and charity works saw to his involvement with pressure groups city-wide, working with the disadvantage ethnic groups, and serving as a governor in primary / secondary / university representing city council also at tribunal appeal.

MEDWAY COUNCIL

COUNCILLOR GLORIA OPARA
Conservative Party; Princes Park Ward;
2015 – Date
Deputy Mayor; 2016/17, 2017/18

Gloria Opara is a dedicated wife, mother of four grown children, and grandmother whose Christian faith propels her to love through service. She is of Ibo descent from the Delta State in Nigeria who moved to the UK in 1985.

She holds a Master's Degree in Information Systems from Canterbury Christ Church University and currently combines her local government duties with a full time lecturing role in Information Technology. Prior to her election as the first black African female member of Medway Council, she held various jobs in Information Technology and finance.

Gloria's wish is that her involvement in public life would leave both a legacy for future generations of young people and inspire others to reach their full potential in life.

CLLR HABEEB ADEYEMI HAROLD OGUNFEMI

Cllr Habeeb Adeyemi Harold Ogunfemi became a parish councillor in Medway Council from May 2011 to date. He started his Primary Education in United Kingdom before relocating to Nigeria with his parents in the 70's where he eventually finished his primary and secondary schools education. Returning to the United Kingdom in 1991, Cllr Ogunfemi attended City of Westminster College where he attained a BTec National Diploma in Business and Finance, and also the University of North London graduating with a BA (Hons) in Business Studies. He is a member of the Chartered Institute of Marketing.

Cllr Ogunfemi has held various positions in different organizations during his education and after graduating from the university. Such positions include: Sales Assistant, Baker, and Departmental Supervisors in different organizations like *LLOYDS TSB*, *HSBC*, *TESCO*, *SAFEWAYS*, etc., Marketing Executive; *POBJOY MINT UK*; Assistant Store Manager, *Lidl Gbmh*; and Team Manager, *National Blood Services*.

Cllr Ogunfemi established the first Afro-

Caribbean Supermarket in Grays, Essex amongst other business ventures which are still in operation till date.

He is Board Member for *Thurrock Racial Unity Support Task Group;* Chairman, *Thurrock Unity Support Task Group*; Director, *The House Of Hope UK* and Vice President, Men's Fellowship (RCCG VFP).

NOTTINGHAM CITY COUNCIL

CLLR LESLIE AYOOLA
Labour Party; Mapperley Ward; 2015 - Date

Cllr Leslie Eni-itan Ayoola was born and raised in Nottingham and the younger brother of Chief Lohofela Ayoola. He has a young daughter by the name of Aseda-Eden Ayoola.

He gained his first degree in Business in 1995 and his Masters degree in Youth & Community Development in 2010.

Cllr Ayoola's 25-year career spans the private, public and voluntary and community sectors, and in 2008 he established Leslie Ayoola Consultancy (a Management Consultancy that provides business support for SMEs and Third Sector organisations). He later went on to set up *Inspiring Greatness* (a social enterprise) specialising in training around Financial Literacy, Employability, Entrepreneurship and Personal Development in 2012 and has been involved in establishing a number of charitable organisations to date.

In his desire to see a fairer society, Cllr Ayoola was elected as a Labour Councillor in Nottingham City for the Mapperley Ward (where he grew up). The Ethnicity break down of his ward according to the 2011 census saw the White British population at 65% and the BME population at 35%.

He is also the Executive Assistant for Business & Employment with addition responsibilities as Director of *EnivroEnergy Limited*, Director of *Marketing NG*, Board Member of *One Nottingham*, Member of the *Audit Committee*, Member of the *Standards Committee* and *Equalities* Board Member

From 2012 to 2016, Cllr Ayoola was a Public Governor for *Nottinghamshire Healthcare NHS Foundation Trust* and prior to this, he became a Joint Audit & Scrutiny Panel Member for the *Nottinghamshire Office of the Police & Crime Commissioner* in 2013.

CLLR PATIENCE ULOMA IFEDIORA

Labour Party; Aspley Ward; 2015 - Date

Cllr Patience Uloma Ifediora was born and raised in Enugu, Nigeria. She graduated with a BA in History and Masters in Political Science and developed a career in the banking industry in Lagos after which she relocated to London in 1998. Following her relocation, she got married and she is blessed with four children.

NOTTINGHAM CITY COUNCIL

Before becoming a Nottingham City Councillor, she worked in the council and with *Eon Energy*. While working at Eon Energy, Cllr Ifediora became a member of the Labour Party in 2011. In 2013 she was selected to be a Councillor and elected in 2015 as one of the Councillors of Aspley Ward in Nottingham City. Cllr Ifediora made history by becoming the first African woman elected as a Councillor in Nottingham City.

As a Councillor, she is a committee member in: *Overview and Scrutiny and Call In Panel, Children and Young People Scrutiny, Health Scrutiny, Corporate Parenting Board, Trusts and Charities* and *Area Committee*. Outside these duties, Cllr Ifediora is a member of the board of directors of *Nottingham City Homes* and *Standing Committee for Religious Education – SACRE*. Cllr Ifediora also represents the Nottingham City Council at *Nottinghamshire Combined Fire Authority*. Cllr Ifediora is actively involved in community events and has also successfully established food bank in various places in Nottingham in collaboration with different local organisations.

OXFORD CITY COUNCIL

Population　　　　　　　　　　151,906

Ethnicity
White
White British　　　　　　　　96,633　　　63.6%
White Irish　　　　　　　　　2,431　　　　1.6%
White Gypsy or Irish traveller　92　　　　　　0.1%
White other　　　　　　　　18,801　　　12.4%

Mixed
White & black Caribbean　　1,721　　　　1.1%
White & black African　　　703　　　　　0.5%
White & Asian　　　　　　　2008　　　　1.3%
Mixed others　　　　　　　　1603　　　　1.1%

Asian or Asian British
Indian　　　　　　　　　　　4,449　　　　2.9%
Pakistani　　　　　　　　　　4,825　　　　3.2%
Bangladeshi　　　　　　　　1,791　　　　1.2%
Asian other　　　　　　　　4203　　　　2.8%

Black or Black British
Caribbean　　　　　　　　　1,874　　　　1.2%
African　　　　　　　　　　4,456　　　　2.9%
Black other　　　　　　　　698　　　　　0.4%

Arab　　　　　　　　　　　922　　　　　0.6%

Chinese or other
Chinese　　　　　　　　　　3,559　　　　2.3%
Other ethnic group　　　　　1,137　　　　0.7%

Source: London Government Directory: A guide to local government in London (2016). London Communications Agency.

CLLR BEN LLOYD-SHOGBESAN

Labour Party; Lye Valley Ward; 2010 - Date

Cllr Ben Lloyd-Shogbesan was elected in 2010, and re-elected 2014 representing Lye Valley Ward in East Oxford, Oxfordshire.

He was previously Vice Chair of *Educational Achievement Committee*, Member *Scrutiny Committee* and *East Area Planning Committee*, *Licensing* and *Gambling Committee*. He was also involved in *Improving Educational Achievements of Black and Minority Ethnic Children* in Oxford City. He is a renowned advocate of encouraging greater participation in council activities for marginalised and minority groups. Cllr Lloyd-Shogbesan has also organised special programmes to celebrate the 1st October Nigerian Independence Day with councillors, the Lord Mayor and members of the Nigerian community

Cllr Ben Lloyd-Shogbesan works for the National Health Service (NHS), and is also a freelance trainer and qualified coach/mentor. He has worked on several international exchange programmes to Eastern Europe (Romania in particular) and to Nigeria on health, social care, community development initiatives and local government and governance issues.

SEVENOAKS DISTRICT COUNCIL

CLLR ANGELA GEORGE
Labour Party; Sevenoaks District Council / Swanley Town Council; 2011 - 2014

Cllr (Mrs) Angela George, the dual-hatted councillor representing Sevenoaks District Council and the Swanley Town Council was elected on the Labour Party platform in 2011. She continues to serve in that capacity till 2014.

Among other positions, Cllr George served as the *Equality and Diversity Officer*, *Labour Group Chair* and the *CLP Executive Committee Member*.

At the district level, Cllr George's committee affiliations included *Housing and Community Safety Advisory, Licensing Committee, Strategy and Performance Advisory* and the *Health Liaison Board* and an *SENCIO Board Member*.

Mrs George's continued community engagement sees her serving variously as a volunteer member of the Communications

Panel at *West Kent Housing Association* and Vice-Chair and Treasurer, *Swanley Whiteoak Action Group*.

Previously an advisor at the Citizens Advice Bureau (CAB), she is still committed to activism as a member of *38 Degrees*, one of UK's biggest campaign communities striving for a more progressive, fairer and better society, and as a collector for the *Swanley Food Bank*.

CLLR ELIZABETH KOMOLAFE
Labour Party, St Mary's Ward; 2015 – Date

Cllr (Miss) Elizabeth Komolafe was elected in 2015 under the platform of the Labour Party to represent St Mary's Ward of the Sevenoaks District Council in the Borough of Bromley. She is a member of the *Finance and Audit Committee* and at times engage in local and international projects.

Cllr Komolafe has a degree in Banking and Finance and has worked with various financial institutions in Nigeria before relocating to the United Kingdom. She has, as a full-time job, been employed by the Halifax Bank PLC since 1999.

THURROCK COUNCIL

Population	157,705	
Ethnicity		
White		
White British White Irish	128,695	81.6%
White other	6,734	4.3%
Mixed	3,099	2%
White & black Caribbean	1,970	0.8%
White & black African	712	0.3%
White & Asian	1,154	0.5%
Mixed others	1,097	0.5%
Asian or Asian British	5,927	3.8%
Indian	5,017	2.1%
Pakistani	1,492	0.6%
Bangladeshi	975	0.4%
Asian other	2,602	1.1%
Black or Black British	12,323	7.8%
Caribbean	2,885	1.2%
African	7,581	3.2%
Black other	1,015	0.4%
Arab	311	0.1%
Chinese or other		
Chinese	1,459	0.6%
Other ethnic group	927	0.6%

Source: London Government Directory: A guide to local government in London (2016). London Communications Agency.

CLLR TUNDE OJETOLA
Conservative Party; South Chafford Ward; 2004 - Date

Cllr Tunde Ojetola, elected in May 2004 on the platform of the Conservative Party, serves as a councillor in Thurrock Council. Ojetola who is Deputy Mayor of the council also serves as the Planning and Regeneration spokesman.

He is a member of the *Planning Committee*, *Children's Scrutiny* and serves as a member on both the *Thurrock Business Forum* and *Dartford Tunnel Improvement Group*.

Cllr. Ojetola is currently Director at both *Impulse Leisure Community Ltd* and *High House Production Park* (Royal Opera House). His works in the area of community engagements, cultural activism and charity works include serving on the *Thurrock Racial Unity Support Taskgroup* (Trust), *Thurrock African Group* and the *Chafford Hundred Community Forum*.

Ojetola won his first election in the South Chafford Ward after the boundary rearrangement in 2004. After being re-elected with an increased majority in 2006, Tunde became a Cabinet portfolio holder, with responsibility for Customer Service, ICT, and e-government.

As a resident of Purfleet, he joined the initial drive to establish the *Purfleet Community Forum*, co-drafting the initial constitution of the Forum and sitting on the Executive Board.

Ojetola now sits on many local organisations and is a spokesman for the local Conservative Party on Planning and Regeneration – which is overseeing a £1bn investment in Thurrock.

Following his tenure as Deputy Mayor, Cllr Ojetola, the Conservative Councillor for Chafford Hundred was recently elected Mayor of Thurrock Council. Becoming the first black mayor of the council, he was sworn in on 24th May 2017.

CLLR BUKKY OKUNADE
Labour Party; Tilbury Riverside and Thurrock Park Ward; 2006 – Date

Cllr. Mrs Bukky Okunade sits in Thurrock Council and has served since first elected in 2006 on the platform of the Labour Party. She currently holds the position of the Cabinet Member responsible for *Children Social Care* in the Council. She also sits on the *Licensing Committee* and as Chair of the *Corporate Parenting Committee*. She was previously member of the *Standards and Audit Committee* of Thurrock Council, *Essex Fire Authority* and *Thurrock Council for Voluntary Service*.

Cllr. Okunade's service in community engagement, cultural activism and charity works has seen her in such roles as co-founder and Chair of *Thurrock African Group* – an organisation formed to provide a forum for African communities in Thurrock, enabling information sharing, and encouraging involvement in projects and initiatives to facilitate community cohesion and linkage with wider Thurrock community.

Bukky's voluntary participation in the community spans the areas of education, housing, racial equality and criminal justice system. She is an active board/committee member of various organisations, such as *Thurrock Racial Unity Support Taskforce*, *Thurrock CVS*, and *Family Mosaic Housing Association* (2003 to 2010). She was a primary school governor with special responsibility for Special Education Needs for a number of years. She has also been involved in the British criminal justice system, having served as a Justice of the Peace (JP) since March 2002.

WATFORD BOROUGH COUNCIL

CLLR FAVOUR EWUDO
Labour Party; 2015 – 2016

Cllr Ifeyinwa Favour Ezeifedi (Ms) was elected in 2015/2016 on the platform of the Labour Party. She was Vice Chair (Membership) of the *Watford Labour Party* and also served on the *Housing* and the *Licensing* Committees.

She is a Parent Governor at the *Grove Academy* which her daughter attends. Favour's working career has spanned the private, public and voluntary sectors. She is currently a team manager in Enfield where her role entails supporting and advocating for vulnerable people with regards to their housing, council tax, benefits, debts management and tenancy sustainment while promoting independence and employability.

Cllr Ewudo is a Trustee of *Aspire Academy Trust* and an active member of both the *African-Caribbean Association* and *Amnesty International*.

WOLVERTON AND GREENLEYS TOWN COUNCIL

CLLR ADEBAYO MURISIKU FASINRO
Labour Party; Stacey Bushes Ward;
2016 – Date

Adebayo Murisiku Fasinro was elected councillor in the United Kingdom. Fasinro, a Muslim from Isale Eko, Lagos Island, joined the growing numbers of other wave-making Nigerians that have been elected into the British political system.

He was elected councillor for Stacey Bushes Ward unopposed to Wolverton and Greenleys Town Council on Thursday 5 May, 2016 under the British Labour Party.

CLLR MUNIR BAKARE
Conservative Party; Greenleys Ward; 2016 to date

Cllr Munir Bakare, the co-opted parish councillor for Greenleys Ward of the Wolverton and Greenleys Town Council is a seasoned educator with specialisations in Early Year, Citizenship, Politics, Government, Special Educational Needs (SEN) and Personal, Social, Health and Economic Education (PSHE).

Having completed an Early Years Professional Programme (EYPS) at the University of Northampton, UK graduating in 2011, Bakare also obtained the Graduate Diploma in Teaching Foundation/Kindergarten and Primary School. His research work was based on Performance Management Review (PMR) and Organisational Theories, and Performance Measurement.

Among other educational institutions, Cllr Bakare has worked at Rainbow Children Centre, Pepper Hill School and Wolverton Day Nursery, both in Milton Keynes .

He is currently working at Rowan Children Centre/Action for Children, Fullers Slade Milton Keynes as a volunteer.

Prior to his current political activism, he had

also worked as a High School teacher for over twenty years and has a Master's degree in Political Science (MA). Although he had one year of a three- year PhD programme in Political Science, the full programmed was not completed, however, due to personal reasons.

In May 2014, he stood for Milton Keynes Council election seat for councillor under the Conservative Party but did not win. He then became a Parish Councillor by co-option for Wolverton and Greenleys Parish Council in November 2016.

His ultimate aim is to eventually stand for political office in Nigeria and work with people to change things for good, help in schools, department of children services, politics, government and citizenship.

Cllr Bakare also looks forward to a future in politics where he can do a lot more to enhance the standard of education through the development of functional curriculum which allow students to achieve their fullest goals.

"In UK politics, everyone is given a chance to prove themselves", he believes. "Politics in Nigeria is on a totally different level, so if we are going to progress politically and make the people feel the benefit of good governance, things will have to change from the status quo."

WYCOMBE DISTRICT COUNCIL

Population   171,644

Ethnicity
White
White British	130,313	75.9%
White Irish	1,553	0.9%
White Gypsy or Irish traveller	103	0.1%
White other	7508	4.4%

Mixed
White & black Caribbean	2259	1.3%
White & black African	328	0.2%
White & Asian	1330	0.8%
Mixed others	932	0.5%

Asian or Asian British
Indian	2939	1.7%
Pakistani	13091	7.6%
Bangladeshi	597	0.3%
Asian other	3009	1.8%

Black or Black British
Caribbean	3382	2.0%
African	1744	1.0%
Black other	808	0.5%

Arab   282   0.2%

Chinese or other
Chinese	949	0.6%
Other ethnic group	517	0.3%

Source: London Government Directory: A guide to local government in London (2016). London Communications Agency.

CLLR SHADE ADOH

Conservative Party; Stokenchurch and Radnage Ward; 2015 -Date

Cllr Shade Adoh (Mrs) was elected councillor in 2015 and is currently Deputy Cabinet Member for Housing. She also serves on the *Independent Review Commission*, and *Personnel and Development Committee*.

Cllr Adoh's varied roles see her serving in the following capacities: Chair, *Nigerian Women in Buckinghamshire*; Board Director, *Healthwatch Buckinghamshire* and Member, *Community Consultative Group on Education, Bucks County Council*.

She is also Chair, *Parents Forum for Children of African & Caribbean Heritage*; Convener, *BME Governors Forum* and School Governor, *Widmer End Combined School*.

Cllr Shade Adoh and her husband (Dr Tonnie Adoh) are passionate about working within the community to encourage cohesion, partnership and youth development, with particular interests in schools and parents working together for the benefit of the child.

THE REPUBLIC OF IRELAND

ROTIMI ADEBARI
Mayor of Portlaoise (2007)
Rotimi Adebari, the Nigerian-born Irish politician arrived in the Republic of Ireland in 2000. As an independent candidate, he was elected into Portlaoise Town Council in 2004. He made history in 2007 when his election as the Mayor of Portlaoise made him the first African to be elected into such position in Ireland.

In the June 2009 Elections, Rotimi retained his Town Council seat and also secured a seat in Laois County Council making him the first and only immigrant to be elected at that level of representation in Ireland. He was a candidate at the 2011 General Elections into the Irish National Parliament (Dail Eireann). Rotimi's background is in sales, marketing and teaching. He obtained a degree in *Economics* from the University of Benin in Nigeria and a Masters in *Intercultural Studies* at Dublin City University, Ireland. He has been a Guest Lecturer in the same university since 2005, teaching managing workplace diversity module.

Rotimi is an Alumni of INSEAD (The Business School for the World) Fontainebleau, France and the Irish Institute at Boston College, Boston, Massachusetts, USA. He has lectured intercultural communication in Champlain College, an American university off-shore campus in Dublin.

Rotimi was a member of the Dublin City University team leading the European Intercultural Workplace Project (2004-2007). The project consortium with its member partners from Ireland, U.K., Bulgaria, Germany, Greece, Finland, Italy, Norway, Poland and Sweden produced reports and training materials to raise awareness and enhance communication between different cultures at work in Europe.

Rotimi served as a jury member for European Programme for Integration and Migration in Brussels. He was a guest speaker to share his thoughts and ideas on what he feels are important for the future well-being of Irish society at the convention on Irish constitutional amendment.

Rotimi, a policy development consultant, an intercultural trainer and a motivational public speaker is the Chief Executive of *Optimum Point Consultancy* – an organisation that specialises in cross-cultural dialogue, capacity building, leadership and workplace diversity Training.

Rotimi pioneered volunteering initiative for National University of Ireland in Maynooth, by promoting volunteering among students and matching them with areas of particular interest. He was responsible for designing integration strategy for immigrants in Laois and coordinated their integration into the wider community.

He was a Director on Portlaoise Educate Together National School Board of Management and Irish National Organisation of the Unemployed. He has also served as a member of Community, Economic Development, Cultural, Heritage, Sport and County Promotion Strategic Policy Committee of Laois County Council.

A Director on the Boards of Laois and Offaly Education and Training Board, Portlaoise Leisure Centre and Dunamaise Arts Centre, in 2006, Rotimi launched an integration initiative called *Voices Across*

Cultures. The initiative uses the attributes of culture namely food, arts and music to promote cross-cultural appreciation on yearly basis in Ireland. Rotimi has also presented a weekly radio show called *Respecting Difference* on *Midlands 103*. The show celebrates cultural diversity and promotes integration.

In his effort to contribute to improvement of learning and research in Africa, Rotimi set up *Books for Africa Ireland*, an Irish not-for-profit organisation. This organisation has donated books to Universities, Polytechnics and Colleges of Education in Nigeria and the Democratic Republic of Congo.

In recognition of his contributions, The Minister for Justice and Equality in 2012 appointed Rotimi a *Peace Commissioner* - an honorary role in Ireland with special powers to primarily taking statutory declarations, witnessing signatures on documents requires by various authorities, signing certificates and orders under various *Acts of the Oireachtas*.

Rotimi has been the recipient of many awards, including: *Social Entrepreneur Award, RTE & Metro Eireann Media and Multicultural Award, Xclusive Magazine Person of the Year, Bold and Beautiful Magazine Person of the Year, Worthy Ambassador* and *Global Achievers Awards*.

Conclusion

This book of profiles is a pioneering effort at its kind of documentation. It beams its searchlight on Nigerian-British politicians in the United Kingdom, both serving and retired. By so doing, the roles and contributions of those involved (first and second-generation Nigerians) are highlighted as a way of documenting this for posterity, and also for referential purposes. It is also hoped that the modest achievements of these forerunners will encourage the coming generations to get more involved and continue the progressive trends.

It is to the credit of the United Kingdom that an enabling environment has not only been created, but also the working modalities of governance have equally allowed the nurturing of aspiring politicians and public administrators. It is an empowering milieu where the Black and Minority Ethnic (BME) politicians continue to contribute and thrive.

With the encouragement of more BMEs to get engaged in the political life of the United Kingdom, comes improved integration and cohesion, which thus foster more positive contributions to the continued development of our adopted country and second home to a lot of Nigerians.

As a pioneer publication, the challenges presented in the course of producing this book can only serve to strengthen future editions, and evolve a robust reference source.

It is not out of place therefore, to infer that *'Nigerian-British Politicians in United Kingdom and Republic of Ireland: A Book of Profiles'* would have kick-started a positive trend whereby diasporic consciousness will encourage diasporas to engage in politics in any part of the world where they reside and influence the policies that affect them positively.